(Left to right) Walton Morris, Chandler Sawyer and Travis Morris smile after a good morning hunt at the Piney Island Club in Currituck County, North Carolina.

Duck Hunting
on Currituck Sound

Tales From a Native Gunner

Travis Morris

THE
History
PRESS

Published by The History Press
Charleston, SC 29403
www.historypress.net

Copyright © 2006 by Travis Morris
All rights reserved

Cover image: (Left to right) Travis Morris handles the shoving pole while his father-in-law, Walton Meiggs, picks up honkers at Cedar Island Bay.

First published 2006

ISBN 978-1-5402-0430-1

Library of Congress Cataloging-in-Publication Data

Morris, Travis.
Duck hunting on Currituck Sound : tales from a native gunner / Travis
Morris.
p. cm.
ISBN 1-59629-167-2 (alk. paper)
1. Duck shooting--North Carolina--Currituck Sound Region--History. 2.
Morris, Travis. I. Title.
SK333.D8M67 2006
975.6'132043092--dc22
[B]
2006020021

This book is dedicated to my Daddy and Mother, Chester and Edna Morris, and my Grandmother Carrie Boswood.

Chester and Edna Morris at Coinjock, North Carolina, in 1950. My mother was born in this house on April 8, 1908. I was born in the same house on November 29, 1932.

Carrie Boswood and Travis Morris in 1950. My grandparents built this house in Coinjock in 1901, the year after they married. Timber for the house was cut from the farm and the labor to build it cost one hundred dollars.

Contents

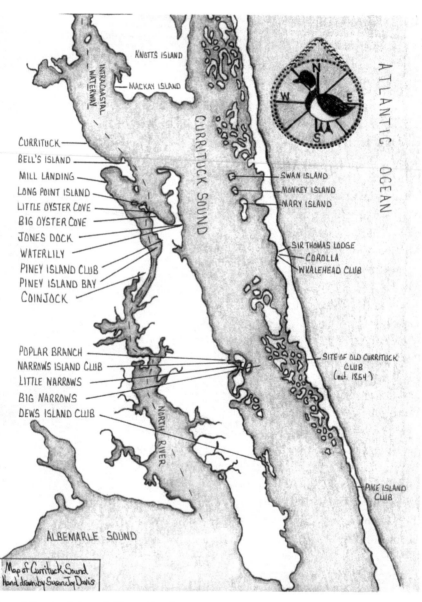

Map of Currituck Sound, North Carolina.

Hunting with Grandad

After counting down every hour until 4:30 a.m., the buzz of the alarm clock finally echoes throughout the room, ending a night of anxiety and restlessness. My grandad, Travis Morris, said he'd pick me up at 5:15, so I'd better be ready at 5:00 because he is always early. I put on my long johns and then the rest of my layers as I see the headlights coming across the backyard. I run downstairs quietly—so as not to wake up Mom and Dad—and grab my gun and gear and throw it in the old Jeep.

The back window on the Jeep doesn't work so I pile my gear in the back seat, being sure to leave a spot for my cousin Chet to sit. I hop in the front seat and fumble around for my seat belt since the interior light only works when you have the right rear door open.

Grandad says, "Hey, bud," and pulls down the driveway as I look at the roof of the old Jeep and see the staples he has shot up there to hold the sagging headliner in place. He has had that old Jeep ever since I can remember, and we still hunt out of it every season.

We pull into Chet's driveway, and he is looking out the door as Grandad chuckles and says, "He's ready, ain't he." Chet shambles out the door with enough gear for all three of us over his shoulder. He manages to find a spot to sit in the gear-laden Jeep, and off we go to our first and most important stop. Now, Grandad has taught Chet and me some vital lessons over the years, but food seems to be the lesson that is taught on every hunting trip. We stop at Kevin's to get a biscuit and some extra nabs for Grandad's already enormous food bag. Kevin says, "Much obliged, fellows," as we head out the door.

When I take my last bite of bacon, egg and cheese biscuit, we arrive at Piney Island where we hook up to the old skiff and put her overboard. Chet and I begin setting our gear on the dock as Grandad pumps up the gas bulb and fires up the old Johnson. Grandad got this skiff for me when I was fourteen years old and, although he has three nicer boats, this skiff is still his pride and joy. She is set up in a traditional Currituck manner with a very appreciated spray hood, a pulley and stick steering system and Grandad's beloved four-horsepower

Johnson, along with an old thirty-five-horsepower Johnson that Mr. DeWitt McCotter gave me when I got the boat. We use that four-horse every time we put out and take up decoys (unless we pole around) and believe me, Grandad's eyes light up whenever he gets the chance to fire the little motor up.

Grandad zips up Old Blue, which is a coat that has seen more hunting days than Chet and I combined. He tells us to put on our life jackets as we push off the dock. I was hunting with Grandad and Mr. DeWitt McCotter one day when Grandad got thrown out of the boat and into the cold water. Luckily, it was shallow enough for him to stand up. Ever since that day we have worn our life jackets while hunting. We leave the basin and start heading north along the Intracoastal Waterway; it is at this point that I feel the cold morning air breeze across my face and realize the rest of the hunting story is irrelevant. Whether we kill a limit of ducks or just get skunked does not matter. We have done both many times. What matters is that Grandad has enough heart to pass on a legacy to Chet and me.

The opportunity to duck hunt with Grandad and listen to all his old tales, as well as take his knowledge and put it to our own use, is a gift beyond measure. Grandad has always made sure we had everything we needed for duck hunting: boats, guns, decoys, shotgun shells, jackets, boots and even down to our socks. He wants us to be ready come hunting season.

Grandad has taught Chet and me many things about the sound and duck hunting. I remember when he was trying to teach me how to pole a skiff. I went around in circles a few times until he had had enough and said, "Just let me show you." Eventually I got the hang of it and I'm glad. Sometimes that's the only way to get back to shore.

Before the season starts, he always makes us help prepare: we tie new decoy lines in the garage or stack them in the boat. He also makes sure we always put everything away after the season ends. If you want to play, you have to work and be responsible.

I have been hunting with Grandad since before I was able to tote a gun, but I didn't see him shoot until a few years ago. I will never forget a hunt we went on together when we rolled out a swan. I told him it was time he shot one. Grandad grinned and pulled the trigger, remarking afterward, "The old boy didn't know what hit him."

There are many small but valuable lessons that Chet and I have learned from Grandad: "Keep your face down" and "Throw the weight into the wind ahead of the decoy" or "Don't quack so much." We've also learned that leaving the dock without a roll of toilet paper is a big mistake. Grandad always said, "You never know when you might have to make a trip to the marsh and bulrushes just don't get the job done."

Travis Morris and grandson Chandler Sawyer poling their skiff to pick up a dead duck at Big Oyster Cove in Cedar Island Bay.

Travis Morris strings up decoys and gets ready for the 1991 season at his home in Maple, North Carolina.

Chandler Sawyer takes a break while hunting with his grandad and West Ambrose at Piney Island Bay.

The three of us have had some great hunts and hunts where nothing would go right. One day we headed home early because it was just a bluebird day with no ducks. On the way, Preston Meekins had a sign in his yard that said, "Ducks for sale." Chet was about seven or eight years old and said, "Let's buy one and shoot him." This tickles Grandad to this day.

I remember my early days of hunting when Grandad and I would carry men across the sound in the *Mother Goose* and tie them out in the float box so they could shoot geese. Grandad would bring a five-gallon bucket of oysters and eat them raw all day long while I shot ducks.

Grandad has had many a nap in the bottom of the blind, but he never misses the chance to be our "retriever" when we shoot a duck down. When Chet and I were younger we had the luxury of tucking up under the spray hood as Grandad braved the freezing wind's spray while running the boat. Things are different now, and guess who is tucked up under that warm hood while we youngsters get a dose of freezing spray.

There is something about Grandad that he probably wishes I wouldn't share. He is a man who knows the sound like the back of his hand and has braved many a cold morning and harsh conditions when most folks would have rather stayed in bed. You would think a man like this would be fearless, but Grandad is petrified of mice. I recall one particular morning when Grandad and I had put the boat over. As we loaded the boat, I saw

Chet Morris keeps watch while having a bite on a cold day in a bush blind on the Intracoastal Waterway at Piney Island.

From the High Blind at Cedar Island Bay, Travis Morris goes to retrieve a teal shot by Chandler Sawyer.

Chandler Sawyer and Chet Morris pose with their bag of mallards after a great gunning day from Laughery Blind at Piney Island.

a mouse scurry under our gear. I knew that if I said something there was a chance he might not go hunting. He would not get in the boat with that mouse. Then I thought to myself, "What's going to happen if we get out in the middle of the sound and he sees that mouse?" Surely I didn't want him to jump overboard or, even worse, try to shoot the little rodent. I decided to inform him of the situation. With a look of near panic and concern, he said, "You're kidding. We're going to have to take another boat." A lot of folks don't have the luxury of taking another boat, but Grandad—being the prepared hunter that he is—was not going to let that mouse get in the way of our duck hunting.

Chet and I have been very lucky boys to have grown up duck hunting with Grandad on Piney Island. He constantly sacrifices for our sake and makes sure that we will have everything we need for future duck hunting when he is gone. We can attribute everything we know about boating and duck hunting to our Grandaddy, including his most important lesson of all: respect the sound. There are times when the sound can be unforgiving, and there is no need in trying her.

We thank the Lord for giving us a Grandaddy who shared all he knows about duck hunting and the sound with us. We can only pray that we will be as giving as he is by passing this tradition on to our grandchildren.

Chandler Sawyer
April 18, 2005

A Love Never Lost

Several people suggested that I write down things I remember about growing up and duck hunting in Currituck. This made me realize that I'm fast becoming one of the older boys; the sun is setting.

I was born in Coinjock, North Carolina, as was my mother, Edna Boswood Morris, and my grandmother, Carrie McHorney Boswood. My great-grandmother was born on Currituck Beach in 1842, so my mother's people have been here a long time.

My love of the water came from my mother's side of the family. Her father was the first mate on a tugboat named the *Nettie*, and her grandfather, Samuel McHorney, was the captain of a sailing ship that traveled to the West Indies. That was during their younger years. When they were older, they came home and farmed.

Travis Morris sporting Old Blue in a duck blind on Currituck Sound.

My father, Chester Ralph Morris, was born in Gates County, North Carolina. He graduated from Wake Forest Law School and came to Currituck to practice law in 1926. That same year, he was appointed county attorney. He was elected district attorney in 1938 and superior court judge in 1947, a position he held until he died in 1973.

During Daddy's years of law practice, he represented most of the old hunt clubs as well as many guides and sportsmen. As a result, he was invited to hunt with these people many times. As his only child, he carried me with him whenever he could. This started my love for duck hunting—a love I've never lost.

Daddy liked to hunt for ducks and quail, but his hand didn't fit a shoving pole. Somebody always had to carry him hunting. By the time that I became a young man, I was the guide for Daddy and his friends.

Duck hunting has been a way of life for me, as it has with a lot of old Currituckers. I've known men employed at the Ford plant in Norfolk, Virginia, who took their vacations during hunting season just so they could guide sportsmen. It's not so much the money as it is a way of life. You meet people duck hunting whom you could not meet any other way. It has been my experience that true duck hunters, regardless of their stations in life, speak the same language and have respect for one another. Therefore, it is my hope that you enjoy the stories bound within this book.

Travis Morris

Why This Book Was Published

This book came about because of Susan Joy Davis, author of *The Whalehead Club: Reflections of Currituck Heritage.* Her book is one that everybody interested in the Currituck Outer Banks should read.

Susan and I spent several days together looking through scrapbooks that my mother, Edna B. Morris, had compiled. During that time, we came across stories that I've written about hunting and fishing over the past thirty years. Susan insisted that they be put together into a book.

I told Susan that there was no way I was writing a book unless it was with her help. I want everybody who reads this book to know that if it were not for Susan Joy Davis, this book would not have happened. She spent countless hours encouraging me in putting these stories together. I'm proud to be able to count Susan and her husband, Bill Davis, as my friends.

Susan Joy Davis enjoys her first boat ride with me on Currituck Sound. The Whalehead Club and Currituck Beach Light are in the background.

My First Hunting Trip, 1938

I was six years old in 1938 when I went on my first hunting trip. The trip was from Bell's Island Club to Thompson Rock, in the north part of Currituck Sound where there used to be many redheads and canvasback.

At the time, Bell's Island was owned by a group of men from New York City. Mr. William S. Gray, who was chairman of the board of Manufacturers Hanover Bank and Trust Company, later bought out the other two members and kept the place as a hunting lodge and Angus cattle farm until his death in the 1960s. Mrs. Gray then sold it to the Ferrell brothers from Currituck County and others for development.

When I first remember Bell's Island, the road was dirt and there were gates on the bridge to keep the cattle in. They ran loose on the marsh at that time. Two large brass eagles sat on the gatepost, but Mrs. Gray later carried them back to their home in Greenwich, Connecticut.

The main hunting from Bell's Island in the early days was from a sink-box called a battery. The club had two battery boats that were thirty-two feet long with little cabins up forward and masts with block and tackle. Both boats had Plymouth car engines and transmissions. The boat basin had a depth of seven feet of water and was bulkheaded up to the shore where there were landing houses used to store decoys. There was also a boathouse where they kept the members' boat, *Bell*. There were three *Bells* that I can remember. I think they brought the first one from New York. It had a varnished cabin that was round in the front and a windshield on the back to protect the helmsman. There were round portholes instead of windows and black leather cushions, and the hull was painted white. It was the prettiest boat I had ever seen.

The procedure was for the guides to go out early in the morning and tie out the rig. Mr. Norman Ballance (who was a good friend of my family) was superintendent of the club. Mr. Norman would know about what time they should be tied out, and he would take the members and guests out in the *Bell* to get into the battery. They would take turns getting in the battery while the

A photograph that was taken thirty-seven years later shows a boat similar to the one from 1938 in which I made my first hunting trip. Pictured is Ambrose "Hambone" Twiford running the old Monkey Island battery boat during the '70s when I operated the Monkey Island Club.

others would stay in the *Bell*'s warm cabin and watch the action. Guides in battery boats would pick up the dead ducks.

At lunchtime Mr. Norman brought members and guests in for a hot meal and short nap at the club. Afterward, he took them back out again, picking them up later in the day. The guides then took up the rigs. Two guides I remember were Mr. Earl Snowden and George Roberts. There were more but I can't recall their names.

By the time I got to go hunting the battery had been outlawed, but the boats were using the same procedure with a lay-down box and later a two-man float box. These were contraptions Mr. Pat O'Neal came up with after the battery was outlawed.

The lay-down box was just like the old lay-down battery except it had sides about ten inches wide that were painted a gray and black camouflage. You set geese around the side of the deck and on the wings. This was a very effective rig for diving ducks; in fact, it was the nearest thing to the old battery there ever was.

To get back to my first day, Mama had laid out all the clothes I could possibly get on (including three pairs of socks). She just knew I was going to freeze to death. We didn't have the warm, lightweight, insulated clothes available now. We had to pile on all the layers we could get around in.

The night before I was so excited I couldn't sleep. Finally, 4:00 a.m. arrived and everybody in the house was up—Mom, Daddy, Granny and me. Granny cooked homemade biscuits and fried ham with red-eye gravy while Mama packed us lunch. Breakfast was over and I was stuffed, so with all the clothes I had on I could barely walk.

I had a single-barrel 410-hammer shotgun. Judge Q.K. Nimmocks from Fayetteville, North Carolina, had given this to me. It had previously belonged to his son Steve. When Steve's son got old enough, I gave it to him.

When we got to Bell's Island I saw the men walking about in the dark with kerosene lanterns. I was so excited I could hardly contain myself. After the usual greetings, Daddy, Mr. Norman, George Roberts, someone whose name I can't remember and me got in one of the old battery boats with the lay-down box on it. We didn't get to go in the *Bell*; only members used that. George tied the skiff with the decoys on while Mr. Norman slipped the old Plymouth in second gear. She had a big wheel so she'd run faster that way. As soon as she warmed up a little, we eased out of the boat basin. Mr. Norman poured on the juice to the old Plymouth, and soon the manifold was cherry red. In those days, with car engines and no water-cooled manifolds, you always took the engine box lid off so it could get some air. The heat from that manifold felt good to cold fingers too. I can hear the exhaust of that Plymouth now and see the steam rising up as we headed down the sound. A lot of canvasback were there. The men put the lay-down box over and then tied out a big stand of ducks and geese.

Daddy probably was the first to get in the box, then Mr. Norman, then me. Of course, I was given all kinds of cautions about what to do and not to do. If Mama had known what kind of contraption I was in, she would have died then and there.

Once in the box, it wasn't long before a booby came up and landed right near my feet. I raised up right easy, cocked my gun, took a bead on the old booby and squeezed the trigger. *Bang!* The old booby fell over dead. At the report of the gun, the gas boat was coming, water flying. I guess they didn't know whether I'd shot a duck or blasted my foot off. Anyway, they got me out and somebody else got in. It wasn't long before we came up on a cripple goose and they let me shoot him from the boat. I pulled the trigger and the old goose fell over. I had shot my first duck and first goose in the same day!

I was ruined for life. I am now seventy-three years old, and to the best of my recollection I have not missed opening day of duck season from that year until now. I loved it so much that Mama and Daddy let me stay home from school on opening days thereafter. In college I cut classes, in the Coast Guard I took leave and since then I have been fortunate enough to be my own boss and haven't had to ask anybody.

Duck Hunting on Currituck Sound

I don't remember how many ducks were killed, but that night after supper we got in the kitchen with a number three washing tub and picked those ducks. We then took a plate off the laundry heater and singed them. By the time I got to bed, nobody had to rock me to sleep; and so it was on my first day of duck hunting.

While I'm writing about Bell's Island, I may as well tell what happened after Mr. Gray died. As I said before, Mrs. Gray sold the property to the Ferrell brothers and others for development, but had a public auction for the personal property. I didn't go because I didn't have any money to buy anything with. Mr. "Lijah" Tate bought five hundred wood ducks for $500. I would love to have had them. Charlie Dozier bought the two-man float box, and the Ferrell brothers bought the only gas boat left, which was a twenty-six-foot tunnel boat Mr. Pat O'Neal had made for Mr. Gray. The boat had no cabin but had a spray hood and a steering wheel mounted on the washboard coaming on each side. I think the boat was the second one like this that Mr. Pat made. It had a concave tunnel that he designed, and it worked better than any tunnel boat I've ever seen. It drew about eighteen inches of water and didn't cavitate like the old box tunnels. The first one of these boats he made was for Mr. Carl White at Pine Island. A Chris Craft engine, which was a 283 Chevrolet block, powered the Bell's Island boat. The Ferrell brothers eventually put a stupid-looking cabin on it. To this day, the boat still sports the same stupid-looking cabin, although a protective canvas was added many years ago. I should know because I put that canvas on when I bought her and changed her name to *Mother Goose*.

At the same time Mr. Pat built this boat, he also built a twenty-three-foot hunting skiff to carry decoys and a float box. Mr. Norman had the sides built high enough so his knees just hit the washboard. This is the best poling skiff I ever tried to pole. Before the sale, Baxter Williams and I made an agreement with Mrs. Gray to keep the skiff for seventy-five dollars. I also offered to carry her and one of her sons and daughters-in-law hunting. This was the last time Mrs. Gray went hunting in Currituck Sound. I still have that skiff: it's sitting under the shelter at Mama's. Just in case the ducks ever come back, it will be ready. The day I was to take the Grays hunting, I got Mr. Pat to go with me to help me handle the rig. I thought Mrs. Gray would enjoy seeing him again. Mrs. Gray was a good shot. We tied her on the Thompson Rock, which is just west of Monkey Island. She killed several redheads that day. Her son was in the box with her, and the daughter-in-law stayed in the boat with us.

I had never carried women hunting before and didn't have any toilet facilities on my gas boat *Rhonda*. The only thing I knew to do was to take a chamber pot. As we got underway that morning, I told them about the pot and if they needed to use it Mr. Pat and I would sit up on the outside of the cabin. The daughter-in-law was pregnant, and it was not too long before she had to use it. All went well until a few minutes later when I looked down and saw water running in the cabin floor. I asked, "Where is all that water coming from?" About that time it dawned on me that the pot must have had a hole in it. I was very embarrassed, but they took it amiably.

My Recollections of Whalehead Club during the 1940s

I believe it was 1939 when Mr. Lindsay Warren was congressman from this district. Daddy got a letter from him asking to get Mr. Callie Parker to take Mr. Ray Adams, who was a meat packer from Washington, D.C., up the beach and show him the Whalehead Club.

Daddy had a 1938 Chevrolet at the time, and on the appointed day when Mr. Adams came, Daddy let me go along. We went to Nags Head and got Mr. Parker, who was to do the driving. When we got to Duck we stopped to let the air down in the tires. The road into Duck was sand too, but you could get that far without letting some air out of the tires. We drove the pole road from Caffey's Inlet to Currituck Club. It was called "pole road" because it followed the old Coast Guard telephone poles. Everybody drove this because the beach was so steep and pebbly, it was hard to drive without getting stuck. When we got to Currituck Club we crossed east toward the ocean and drove north to Corolla. The sand flattened right out and was the prettiest beach I had ever seen. It was almost like driving on a paved road.

At this point, I think I need to tell you how the Whalehead Club came to be. (For even more details, I suggest you read *The Whalehead Club: Reflections of Currituck Heritage* by Susan Joy Davis.) The club, formed by a group of men from Boston and New York, originated in 1874 and was known as the Light House Club of Currituck Sound. On November 26, 1919, the property was sold to Leroy W. Davis, William A. Davis and Clyde L. Davis. Then in 1922, Mr. Edward Collings Knight Jr. of Newport, Rhode Island, and Philadelphia, Pennsylvania, bought the Light House Club property. Mr. Knight was an executive with the Pennsylvania Railroad. His second wife, Marie Louise LeBel Knight, was French Canadian. She was quite a character from what I have heard from the people who knew her. Mr. Knight had hunted from the Light House Club in previous years, but the members would not allow women to hunt at the club. Since his wife liked to hunt, when Mr. Knight got an opportunity to buy the property he did so and built an elegant home. The five-chimney house was built on a little island to the northwest of the old Light House Club. He had it dredged out around the island to make a high hill on which to build his house. Mr. Knight called this Corolla Island and built two arched bridges for access.

The lodge was started in 1922 and completed in 1925 at a cost of $383,000. (This figure was given to me by Mr. Johnnie Austin of Corolla, who was informed by Mr. Knight's bookkeeper.) The building has twenty rooms and ten full baths, plus two half-baths, on the three main floors. There are sixteen rooms in the basement. The roof is copper and the pipes are all brass, the floors are cork and the chandeliers are signed and numbered Tiffany glass. There is also an elevator.

Mr. Knight died July 26, 1936, and Mrs. Knight died October 29, 1936. In Mr. Knight's will, he appointed the Pennsylvania Company as trustee for his estate. The Corolla property was put up for sale since his heirs were all women who were not interested in hunting. Mr. Lindsay Warren had visited the estate and spoke about it in Washington. A wealthy congressman from New York State named Sirovich made them an offer of $175,000. The day Sirovich was to close the transaction he died. Mr. Ray Adams was also a friend of Mr. Warren and learned about the property.

When we arrived at Corolla Island, I believe it was Mr. Cleveland Lewark who was the caretaker and showed us around. I remember going to that clubhouse the first time. All the furniture was normally covered with white sheets, but was uncovered for Mr. Adams's inspection. I remember a grand piano, two grandfather clocks and a safe with ducks and other wildlife on it that had come from the old Light House Club. The dining room had a long table and a long buffet. I remember a bellows by one of the fireplaces, a leather couch and pretty chandeliers. That's all I remember about the furnishings. As a seven-year-old boy I wasn't too interested in the decorations.

After our tour, Mr. Adams returned to Washington and made an offer of $25,000 for the property with a $2,500 down payment and the balance in nine years at 4 percent interest: quite a contrast to its present value. On August 20, 1940, Mr. Herbert O. Frey, vice-president of the Pennsylvania Company, wrote Mr. Adams telling him their trust committee had approved his offer for the property, which consisted of the clubhouse and approximately two thousand acres of land with about four-and-a-half miles fronting the Atlantic Ocean and Currituck Sound. Because my daddy represented Mr. Adams, I had this letter on file until my office burned in 1980.

Mr. Adams named the place Whalehead Club and employed Captain Neal Midgett and his wife Miss Daisy to oversee it. They were from Nags Head and owned the First Colony Inn. Mr. Adams used the club to entertain his friends and customers. After one season, Captain Neal and Miss Daisy left and Mr.

An aerial view of the Whalehead Club at Corolla during the 1940s.

Adams employed Mr. Dexter Snow as superintendent. He stayed until after Mr. Adams's death on December 31, 1957, and retired in 1958. Gene and Shirley Austin lived in Corolla and were employed after Mr. Snow's retirement. They stayed there longer than the other caretakers who worked there.

On August 6, 1942, Mr. Adams leased the property to the U.S. Coast Guard. Part of the arrangement was that Dexter Snow be made chief bos'n mate and that he be stationed at Corolla to look after Mr. Adams's interest. At this time, the Coast Guard had as many as three hundred men housed there. After the war, Mr. Adams turned it back into a hunting lodge.

Many distinguished guests enjoyed the grandeur of the lodge. At a beach party Mr. Adams held in June 1942, the guests included: former North Carolina Governor O. Max Gardner; Speaker of the House Sam Rayburn of Texas; Senator Walter R. George of Georgia; Lewis Deschler of the House of Parliament; Vice-Admiral Russell R. Waesche, commandant of the U.S. Coast Guard; comptroller general of the United States, Lindsay C. Warren; Congressman Herbert C. Bonner; Congressman Sterling Cole of New York; and Congressman Graham Borden of New Bern. Other members of the party were retired U.S.C.G. Admiral L.C. Covell, Judge Frank Robertson of Mississippi, U.S. Marshall Ford S. Worthy of North Carolina and District Solicitor Chester Morris.

Left to right: Chester Morris and Travis Morris return home to Coinjock after a successful hunting trip at Whalehead in 1949.

There were many others who enjoyed Mr. Adams's hospitality. Among them were the Superior Court judges of North Carolina, who held their annual conference there in 1948. In addition, the members of Boy Scout Troop 172, sponsored by Pilmoor United Methodist Church of Currituck, will always remember Mr. Adams and Corolla. For two summers he gave us a week at the beach and let us stay in the Currituck Beach Coast Guard Station, which he then owned. The food we were served and the good times we had will not be forgotten.

Mr. Adams would stop by our house to talk business with Daddy at times when he was on his way to Corolla. He and my grandmother Carrie Boswood, who was many years his senior, became great friends. The summer before Mr. Adams died in 1957, he sent a boat to Waterlily to carry Granny, who was eighty-four years old at the time, to Whalehead to have lunch with him. She enjoyed going there again since her two grandfathers, Abraham Baum and Samuel McHorney, had both owned much of this land through land grants from the state of North Carolina dating back to 1830.

As a young boy I went duck hunting with Daddy at Whalehead Club on several occasions. There were usually a lot of people there, and most were either senators or congressmen or Coast Guard admirals. On the afternoon of the hunt, we would go to Poplar Branch Landing to meet the boat. Whalehead, Currituck and Pine Island Clubs all left from Poplar

Branch Landing. Mr. Norman Gregory ran a store there that supplied all the clubhouses. He even ran a barge to haul coal for the furnaces and corn to feed the ducks. Mr. Dexter Snow would be there to meet us with the old shad boat, loaded with supplies and baggage.

It was about six miles across and up Currituck Sound from Poplar Branch to Corolla. When we got to Whalehead, it would be getting late in the afternoon, and there would usually be a big bunch of canvasback out by the end of the point as we headed in the channel to the club. Mr. Adams fed ducks there without hunting them so people could see them from the big picture windows in the living room. When we docked in the basin somebody would be there with an old army truck to take the bags up to the house. There was a command car for guests to ride in.

When we got inside the house, there were roaring oak fires in the fireplaces. After everybody settled in their rooms, the men had drinks and it would soon be time for dinner. Afterward, the men sat around to spin yarns until bedtime. By 8:30 p.m. Mr. Adams would tell his guests to stay up as long as they wanted to, but he was going to bed. During the night I was so excited anticipating the next day's hunt that I hardly slept. At about 5:00 a.m., somebody knocked on the door and told us it was time to get up.

We got up and went down to the dining room for a big breakfast. Daddy taught me a lesson at that dining room table that I still remember to this day. We had biscuits, and when they passed the jelly I put it on my biscuit using the spoon in the jelly instead of the one on my plate. Daddy corrected me. It embarrassed me, and I've never forgotten.

After breakfast we walked to the dock in front of the club. The guides had tied several skiffs behind each gas boat and dropped them off at various blinds. At lunchtime the gas boats came by to pick everybody up for lunch. After lunch and usually a nap, we went back out to hunt until take up time at 4:20 p.m. I saw as many as one hundred ducks and geese at the game room in the boathouse.

For some reason, Mr. Adams seemed to take a liking to me. One morning he sent Jarvis Snow to pick me up at Poplar Branch. I was supposed to have lunch with him and hunt that afternoon.

Jarvis had what was then called a speedboat. It was an open boat about twenty feet long with a flat head V8 Ford motor. The engine was decked all the way across, making two cockpits. The steering wheel was on the back of the engine box, and that boat probably did a little more than thirty miles per hour. At the time, there were several boats around Poplar Branch Landing built like that. On Sunday afternoons in the summer they had races in Dowdy's Bay near Grandy.

Mr. Ray Adams leaves for Washington, D.C.

To get back to hunting, Mama carried me to Poplar Branch that morning, and as I said, Jarvis was there to meet me. I remember it was a clear, cold morning. That same day Daddy was hunting down on the Narrows Island property with Mr. Orville Woodhouse.

We got to Corolla and I followed Mr. Adams around until lunchtime. Several senators and the commandant of the Coast Guard were there. Mr. Adams got a call and had to return to Washington immediately, spoiling our hunting trip. He told me I could stay and one of the guides would take me hunting or he would send me down to the Narrows where Daddy was. I decided to go to the Narrows. Mr. Dexter Snow took us in that boat of Jarvis's because it was fast. He dropped off Mr. Adams at Poplar Branch where his car was and then decided he had better find somebody in Mr. Jerry Bunch's store to go with him through the Narrows, as it had been a long time since he had been through there. It's deep water if you know where you are going, but if you don't, there's no water at all. He found somebody, and we went to one of the marsh guard camps to find out which pond Daddy and Mr. Woodhouse were in. The clubs in those days all had guard houses on the marsh and employed guards to stay there day and night during the hunting season. Their job was to keep poachers away.

When we got to the pond, Daddy put me in the blind with Mr. Woodhouse. We kept hearing honking but couldn't see a goose. Finally, I looked down and saw that the goose was right beside us. At that very moment the goose flew away. We both emptied our guns but never touched him. I guess he was just too close.

The Wharf at Currituck

When I was growing up there were two long wharves at Currituck where the ferry dock is now. The longest one was the County Wharf that extended about five hundred feet and then had a thirty-degree turn to the south with an additional one hundred feet of length. Five or six fish houses sat on the wharf's north side, one of which was in the bend of the wharf. In the hot summertime a lot of us boys got running starts from atop those fish house roofs to dive over the wharf and into Currituck Sound. This was dangerous, but I don't recall anybody getting hurt.

Fishermen stored their nets at these fish houses. In those days, nets were made of cotton and were tarred so they wouldn't rot. I loved to smell the fragrance of that tarred rope during the fall when fishermen sat in the lee of the fish houses to mend net in a cold northeaster. There were also several carp pens where the fish were held until tank trucks routinely arrived from New York to buy them.

About 150 feet south of the County Wharf was another, not quite as long, called Johnson's Wharf. This belonged to Mr. Ed Johnson and was right behind his store. It had a carp pen at the end. There was a deep hole between the bend of the County Wharf and Johnson's Wharf. This was a favorite swimming hole of the boys and girls in the community. Sometimes on a sizzling summer day some of us boys went to the Wharf to go swimming but did not have our bathing suits. With nobody else around, we just pulled our clothes off and jumped in. One day when we did this some people drove up in a car. We stayed in the water for about an hour until they left.

One summer day Billy Simpson and I went crabbing down at the Wharf and collected about a bushel of hardcrabs. We carried them up to the courthouse and turned them loose in the Register of Deeds office, where Miss Edna Blossom worked with another woman. We boys were delighted at the mischief we had made: imagine those hardcrabs running all over the floor snapping and the two women screaming. Miss Edna told me in no

Currituck Wharf circa 1955. From this location today, the Knott's Island Ferry arrives and departs.

uncertain terms to get those crabs out of there before she called Daddy. We gathered the crabs up.

Back then there were several long nets fishing out of Currituck. Charlie Snowden had three rigs, and Mr. Earl Snowden, Mr. Lou Brumsey, Mr. Wallace Davis and Mr. Charlie Simpson each had one. I also remember the old battery box that Mr. Tom, Frank and Carl Brumsey used to hunt rested on the shore near the head of the wharf.

Years before my time the wharf went out to what we call the pier head, where there was a bunch of old pilings just about water level. I guess this was where sailing ships tied up when they passed through Old Currituck Inlet to the Port of Currituck during the 1700s and early 1800s.

Memories of Mill Landing in Maple, North Carolina, during the 1930s and 1940s

Mill Landing is the place at Maple where the water comes right up to the road. There is a piece of land right across the creek from the bait shop that still belongs to the heirs of what was known as the Maple Warehouse Company. This company was formed before my day by a group of farmers. They dredged a channel and built a warehouse so freight boats could get their potatoes and other produce to carry it to Norfolk. From there it was probably shipped by rail to Northern markets since there was no trucking industry back then.

I can remember the warehouse and the docks. In fact, I kept a boat there for nearly twenty years. One man built row skiffs there for somebody in Ocean View who rented them out. I was six years old at the time and I had constructed a boat out of a dry goods box and put it in the ditch in the pasture. I stuck a blind and had some decoys that my grandaddy had given me. Mama said Daddy told her if I wanted a boat that badly he was going to buy me one. He bought the last skiff the boat's builder made before he died. Daddy paid twenty-five dollars for it. It was made for rowing, so Daddy asked his friend Buck Allen to put hobbles on it, and then Daddy installed a Water Witch outboard motor.

Years passed, then Mr. Earl and Charlie Snowden started hunting out of Mill Landing. This was before they used a float box. They lodged sportsmen in the old Snowden house on Maple Road and carried them to bush blinds in open water, mainly out on Great Shoal. They used the old Tom Brumsey battery boat. She was built by Mr. Wilton Walker and was thirty-two feet long. She had a fairly good-sized cabin up forward with a bench seat on each side. The rest of the boat was open, and she was steered with a tiller.

Henry Doxey ran this boat for them, and I have seen her leave Mill Landing with seven skiffs in tow. He would tow them out to the shoal and drop off a skiff, two sportsmen and a guide. The guide had no outboard motor, just a shoving pole. He'd go to the next blind and repeat the process until he had cut them all loose. In the afternoon he would go back around and pick them all up again and start for home. By the time they got back to Mill Landing, it was after dark.

One day they were out there and a bad storm blew up. Henry gathered up his men, but it was blowing so hard that most had to leave their decoys. Henry also picked up other people in small boats who were in trouble. By this time, the old gas boat was loaded so heavy she was taking on quite a bit of water. Guides took turns pumping as hard as they could, and some of the sportsmen got scared and wanted to know where the life preservers were. When the guides said there weren't any, they really panicked. After they had safely reached the shore, some of the sportsmen reported it to the Coast Guard. As a result, the Coast Guard required a special test for Currituck Sound guides held in Griggs School. I took it at one point and wish I had kept that license. It was a unique situation because they only tested that one time and afterward never required such testing for guides.

At Mill Landing, there was an old man named Buck Allen who lived on a houseboat. He later lived there in an old shack. He was the one who put the hobbles on my first skiff and later made me decoys out of fence posts. He and I became good friends because I hung around there so much. He was the cussingest man I ever knew. Sometimes he was so bad I didn't like to be with him, like early one morning when I caught him cussing the Lord. The tide had come up in a pen where he had some ducks, and it was so cold it had frozen them right in their tracks. He was out there pulling their feet out of the ice. I just went back to my boat and went hunting.

"Captain" Buck had a little skiff with a Minus inboard motor. He would crank that thing and when it wouldn't start, he got so mad he unbolted it and threw it overboard. The water where he threw it was shallow and after he cooled off, he'd get it out, put it back on the boat and get it going for a while. He did this at least three times when I knew him.

I kept my first, second and third gas boats at Mill Landing. I got my first gas boat when I was fifteen years old. I convinced Mama and Daddy to let me rob my savings account of $350, which was all I had, to buy an old boat from Vernon Lee Creekmore who lived in the north part of Currituck Sound near the launch. Daddy took me up there with Ben Taylor on a Sunday afternoon to get it.

The boat had an old Model A Ford motor in it. The battery was dead, but it had a crank; Vernon Lee said that after we got it running the generator would keep it going. It was a clear, calm Sunday afternoon and that old

Ben Taylor sits with a surfboard on the bow that his brother Wayne made. It had a wooden frame covered with canvas and was the first surfboard I'd ever seen. We used it to ride waves in the ocean, and we pulled each other on it behind my first gas boat with a Model A Ford motor, which is shown in this circa 1950 photograph with me standing at the tiller.

The *Sea Lizard* after I bought her in 1952.

Model A was clucking. At fifteen, I really thought I was something standing back at the tiller of that big boat. She was twenty-one feet.

Everything was fine until we got off Bell Point, when the generator quit genning and the Model A quit clucking. Now the trouble began because the water was deeper than my shoving pole and the wind was dead calm. The only solution I knew was to throw the anchor as far as Ben and I could and pull it in. This was slow going, but luck turned out to be with us. Jack Privott had stopped at the end of Currituck Wharf with his binoculars and saw us. He then went to Mr. Earl Snowden who took his gas boat out to get us. To say we were glad to see him is an understatement.

The next fall when I got my driver's license, I built a dock right beside the highway so I could just get out of the car and in the boat. I always left all my gear, decoys and everything right there beside the road. Back then we knew everybody, and if anyone stole anything you most likely knew who it was.

I kept this boat several years before I traded it to Marson Roberts for an old boat they called the *Sea Lizard*. She had a flat rocking chair bottom, a cabin with windows all around and a shelter cabin. She was powered with a flathead V8 Ford motor hooked up straight. Charlie Snowden had this boat built in the Rehobeth Church yard the year President Roosevelt went to see the Lost Colony. I think it was 1937.

I kept the *Sea Lizard* until several years after Frances and I were married. I had many good times with this boat, mostly hunting in Coinjock and Cedar Island Bays. By then I had two duck blinds that Mr. Norman Ballance had given me. Mr. Norman also gave me decoys: twenty-five old ducks and twelve geese. By this time, Mr. Gray was just using the float box, and the game board had made a ruling that clubs couldn't have open water blinds in their names. Instead they had to be in the name of a county resident, and I was more than willing to accept them.

When Frances and I were first married, her daddy, Mr. Walton Meiggs, had a float box that Edgar O'Neal's daddy (Mr. Pat O'Neal's brother) had built for him. At the time it was built Edgar had a gas boat, but he sold it and Mr. Walton wasn't using the float box. I inherited it because the only thing he had to carry it on was a sixteen-foot skiff, which wasn't nearly big enough.

I remember one Thanksgiving Day when Rives Manning, my cousin from Roanoke Rapids, was with me and we tied out in Bellows Bay. (This is near what is now the Knott's Island Ferry Landing; however, there was no ferry then.) The wind breezed up about twenty-five miles per hour from the northwest. We had just gotten all the decoys taken up and the box loaded and tied down when the skiff suddenly sank. Of course, she didn't go to the bottom because she was wood, as were all the decoys and the float box. There was nothing else to do but tow it back to Mill Landing with decoys floating everywhere. I think that was the most tangled up mess I have ever seen.

Back when I was fifteen, Daddy was holding court all over the eastern part of the state. He went as far as Burlington and down to Wilmington. People knew he was from Currituck, and I guess they thought the place was working alive with ducks. They always wanted to come home with him to go duck hunting so we had many visitors. I was recruited into guide service from the time I was fifteen years old until well after Frances and I were married. Granny's house was like a free hunting lodge, and everybody was always made to feel welcome and at home, regardless of their station in life. Granny would be up early mornings cooking fried ham, homemade biscuits and red-eye gravy, while Mama packed the lunches.

On one of these occasions I got Mr. Walton to go with me to help with the box. There were many canvasbacks in Coinjock Bay that year, and we were tied down in the southern part of the Bay just off Bear Point (off against where Piney Island Club is now).

I was sick with a cold and felt terrible. When the time came to go home, it was slick calm and spitting a little rain. Mr. Walton and I decided to leave the rig out that night and come back the next day to get it. We had about 125 ducks out and 40 or 50 geese. That night the wind blew fifty miles per hour and the tide carried our ducks through Coinjock Canal. Elijah Tate said he saw them just sailing through the canal. He picked up some and gave them back to me. We picked up all we could find but lost I don't know how many. That taught me another valuable lesson: never leave decoys out overnight.

Before I had my driver's license, Mama would take me up to Mill Landing and leave me for the entire day. I spent many good times there.

Mr. Pat O'Neal and Archie Midgett

M r. Pat was a little Irishman with a lot of wit. He was a great waterman as well as one of the best boat builders in this area. All the major hunting clubs except Whalehead had boats Mr. Pat built. Mr. Adams wouldn't pay the price that Mr. Pat charged. When I can first remember Mr. Pat, he carried sportsmen during the hunting season, fished with a long net until springtime and then built boats until the season began again. He was chairman of the Currituck County Game Board for many years.

The first job I ever had was painting boats for Mr. Pat. He had a shop on the canal bank at Coinjock where the north part of Harrison's Marina is located today. I can still smell those juniper shavings and hear Mr. Pat talking about engines with chinaware sparkplugs. I heard many yarns spun there.

I remember one story about when he was market hunting with somebody. It was a time before gas boats, when they had a sailboat to carry the battery and wait on the rig. There was a very specific way to switch men in and out of the battery: the man in the boat would sail by and jump in the battery simultaneously as the man in the battery would jump in the boat. Well, Mr. Pat sailed by and jumped in the battery but the other man failed to jump in the boat in time, so they were both in the battery with the boat sailing off. Now mind you, that was not the most immediate problem. With both men in the battery, it was going to sink fast if they didn't do something. The only thing to do was start throwing the forty-pound weights overboard. Thankfully, another hunter saw the empty boat sailing and rescued them.

Mr. Pat invented the two-man sit-up box after the old battery was outlawed. I still have the one that Mr. Walton Meiggs had. I also have a lay-down box that Mr. Pat made for Mr. Walton and I. Mr. Pat also came up with this contraption when they outlawed the lay-down battery. The box was level with the water. The rig had a board about ten inches high, painted black and gray camouflage and geese decoys were set all around it. This was the most deadly redhead and canvasback rig I have ever seen. I still have it.

Mr. Pat hunted with Mr. Walton and me quite a bit in later years, after he had quit guiding. He was one of the best shots I ever encountered.

One day when I was working for Mr. Pat, I had gone home to dinner while Mr. Pat stayed at the shop. The phone rang and his wife Mrs. Madeline said, "Travis, go to the shop and get Pat. He has always wanted to kill a deer and there are two in the pea field beside the house." I did as she said as quickly as possible. When we got back to the house, Mr. Pat got out two guns: one for him and one for me. We crawled down the ditch until we were within range. Mr. Pat killed the buck. The doe came within fifteen feet of me but I just couldn't pull the trigger on her. I have never killed a deer and have no desire to do so.

While I'm on the subject of Mr. Pat O'Neal, I need to tell you about Archie Midgett, who was Madeline's first cousin. Archie was a retired bachelor, and he stayed with Mr. Pat and Mrs. Madeline. He was the most peculiar person I think I have ever known, yet very likeable. He said he could tell if milk had ever been in a cup or glass and if it had, he wouldn't drink from it.

Archie stayed around the boat shop all the time and he wanted to rig up a fishing rig. He got Mr. Pat to build him two wide, identical flat-bottom skiffs about twenty-two feet long. He put a motor in one and the other he used for a fishing skiff. The one with the motor was, years later, lengthened and a cabin was put on it.

One winter Mr. Wallace Davis, who was a good long net fisherman, Bill Snowden and I ran a long net rig of Archie's. We had thirteen hundred yards of net. We made two or three hauls a day and many times had to take money out of our own pockets to pay the gas bill. I know that net must not have been hung to fish the bottom because other rigs fished right around us and caught fish while we couldn't catch very many. Mr. Wallace was captain, Bill pulled the cork line and I pulled the lead line.

When the weather got warm, we had to put the carp in what we call a "carp car." This was a little skiff with a top on it and two doors in the top. It was bored full of one inch holes to keep the carp alive. When we got to Mr. Casey Jones's dock we had a ramp we would pull the carp car on, count them and weigh them, then throw them in the carp pen until a tank truck came to carry them to New York.

The first summer that Frances and I were married, I was working at Mr. Pat's and Archie had rigged up a mullet net. This was before the days of monofilament when you had to mullet fish at night; otherwise, the fish would see the net and wouldn't go in it.

After I got off work some afternoons, Archie and I and whomever else we could find—sometimes my friend Ambrose "Hambone" Twiford and sometimes Mr. Walton—would go fishing. I remember one particular occasion in September 1954, when Archie, Mr. Walton and I went mullet fishing. When I finished work, we left Mr. Pat's shop and went through the ditch beside Churches Island Road and out Parker's Creek to the sound. We crossed the sound to Parker's Bay. The object was to get over there just before dark so we could see the mullets jumping and know where to set the net. This net was about 125 yards long. We got it overboard and waded it around. We also had a six-volt light bulb that we tied on the top of a shoving pole. We hooked it up to a battery so we could see how to take the fish out. The mosquitoes were so thick you could take your hand and wipe layers off your arms once in a while.

We made this haul in Parker's Bay and caught more carp than we did mullets. This was a mess because they got caught by their dorsal fins and were hard to get out of the net. After we got through with the carp, we went over to Shipp's Bay and really got in the mullet. I think we caught about three boxes, and these were big mullets.

Now it came time to start home and it was dark as pitch. There were not a lot of lights on the shore like there are now. Archie had no sense of direction, but you couldn't tell him anything. He thought he knew where he was going. When we got to the west side of the sound, we were at the north end of Churches Island instead of the south end where we wanted to be. This meant we had to run parallel all the way down the island around the south end to get to Parker's Creek. Just as we got to the little bridge, the old engine coughed a few times and then died. That was it. She was out of gas. It was 1:00 a.m.

To Mr. Pat's shop where our cars were, it was four or five miles because we had to go all the way to Coinjock bridge, cross the bridge and then head back to Mr. Pat's shop. The only way to get there was to walk, so we did. Mr. Walton and I had long legs but Archie's were short, and we nearly walked him to death. We would have to stop once in a while and let him rest. We finally got to the shop and got transportation to get gas, and then we had to carry our fish to Elizabeth City. That was some ordeal.

Rhonda the Gas Boat, 1961 to 1985

I think I can safely say I've had more enjoyment out of this boat than any hunting boat I've ever had. Riley Beasley of Coinjock built this boat in 1947 for his brother, Elwood. Originally, the boat had a spray hood instead of a cabin and was painted white. She had a deep deadrise bow and tumblehome stern. She was named *Betty Ann*, and I thought she was a very pretty boat. I used to ride over to Churches Island and see her tied off to a stake in front of Mr. Beasley's house.

At the time, the boat had a six-cylinder Chevrolet engine, hooked up straight with no transmission, and I'd been told it would run thirty-three miles per hour. She was the fastest on the island until Mr. Pat O'Neal built one for Bill Twiford that would beat her. Soon after the *Betty Ann* lost her title, Mr. Beasley had Grissie Barco put a cabin and little shelter cabin on her: when she was no longer the fastest boat on the island he preferred a little more weight and comfort.

When Mr. Beasley died, Mrs. Beasley had *Betty Ann* put in the ditch beside Churches Island Road with a for sale sign. I called her up and she wanted $1,000 for the boat. To me, that amount may as well have been $10,000. It was just out of my reach. That boat sat there for a whole year until one night, in the fall of 1960 or '61, I was reading the paper and saw it advertised for $400. I had just picked and sold my soybeans, and after I read that ad, I went right over there and gave Mrs. Beasley four $100 bills. I was happy as a cat with two tails.

The engine hadn't been started in a year, so the next day I got a mechanic (I think it was Joe Ringer) to go over there with me to get her. A little gas in the carburetor, a new battery and filed points and she fired right up. I brought her back to Mill Landing where I kept her for about a year. In honor of my daughter, I changed her name from *Betty Ann* to *Rhonda*.

The first day of hunting the next year, Mr. Pat O'Neal, Mr. Walton and I were hunting in the sound off Corolla. It was too far to go back to Maple so we decided to go into Mr. Casey Jones's dock at Waterlily and see if he would

Herbert Lange and Travis Morris with a decoy skiff at tow behind the *Rhonda* and a float box tied out on Thompson Rock, southwest of Monkey Island. Wilson Snowden took this photograph around 1969.

let us tie up there. He did and I made a deal with him to keep the boat there. I kept it there for as long as I owned the boat, which was until 1984 or '85. Mr. Casey and I also began a friendship that lasted as long as he lived.

The next year, I got Mr. Pat to put a new shelter cabin on her. Then I put side curtains and a rear curtain on. I got a little gas heater and you could take your coat off in there most any day. I ran this boat many, many miles, particularly during the days of the "Roving Hunters." When the Chevrolet gave out, I put a 442 Oldsmobile in it. With this engine, it would take that twenty-three-foot skiff I got from Mrs. Gray, two hundred wood ducks, eighty geese, the float box and seven people in the gas boat, and she'd pop it all right out on top and go with it. I later went through two 318 Chrysler Marine engines. Both were used, but the last one was a very good engine.

In addition to all my hunting, owning the *Rhonda* aided the development of Corolla Village starting in 1971. I carried people across Currituck Sound in this boat and sold oceanfront lots for $12,000. This boat enabled me to do what other real estate people couldn't: I could get people to Corolla in about twenty minutes in reasonable comfort and in any kind of weather.

When I was running Monkey Island Club, I used this boat everyday. I also used this boat in the process of selling Monkey Island. Such people as Timothy Mellon (Paul Mellon's son) and William F. Rockwell (who at the time was chairman of the board of North American Rockwell) rode in this boat. The day the Mellon Foundation Trustees were at Monkey Island, I think the tide was as low as I ever saw it. I couldn't get the gas boat closer than one hundred feet from the dock. I had to take my big twenty-three-foot hunting skiff to get the people from the boat to the dock, and then have a ladder for them to get on the dock. I also carried them to the dock at the end of the airstrip at Whalehead Club where I had three jeeps waiting to show them the beach. Each time that I transported them from the boat to shore, Mr. Rockwell realized the adverse circumstances and would tell me, "Well done." As a result of this tour, the Mellon Foundation gave the Nature Conservancy $4 million to buy Monkey Island and Swan Island. At the time, this was the largest cash grant ever given to a conservation organization.

We sold Monkey Island in 1978 so I had no further use for the boat there. Duck hunting in the sound was so poor that nobody wanted to go to the trouble of putting out the float box. I had sold out Corolla Village and had bought a thirty-five-foot Pacemaker motor yacht to satisfy my boating needs in 1979.

For the next three to four years, the *Rhonda* just sat at the dock with seldom use. One January morning when the sound was frozen and the temperature was in the teens, I was in Elizabeth City trying to get the blower on my furnace fixed when I got a call from Jimmy Jones saying my boat was sunk. I called Jimmy at Piney Island Club and asked him to get Hambone and start pumping the water out of the *Rhonda*. I got there as soon as I could, and they said the water had been over the top of the carburetor and of course, was in the engine. I had just put a new carburetor on it, but it had sunk because water had frozen in the exhaust pipe and burst a hole in it. I said, "Somebody else is going to own this boat before the sun sets tonight because I'm going to give it to somebody." Mr. Frank Carter was standing there and said, "Call Walton Carter. He will take it." That is what I did—and walked away from it.

There is one more story about the boat *Rhonda*. Mr. Charles Simpson was a retired grocery store owner. He had been helping me guide at Monkey Island. After the hunting season in 1978, he was doing some trapping so I let him trap the Monkey Island marsh. Late one foggy afternoon in January, his wife Miss Katherine called me and said he had not come home from trapping. It was getting late and she sounded worried about him. She asked if I would go look for him, and of course I told her I would. Their son, Billy Simpson, my son, Walton Morris, and Hambone went with me to look for him. Later in the evening Miss Katherine called the Coast Guard.

I thought maybe Mr. Simpson's motor broke down and that he had poled to a duck blind. It was foggy so I went to Monkey Island first. From Monkey Island I had compass bearings to blinds that I thought he might be in. As night came so did a gale of wind out of the southeast and the fog lifted. We went to all the open water blinds where we might find him with no luck. Then we looked around the marsh. By then, the Coast Guard caught up with us. They had an inflatable boat with an outboard motor.

Remember, we had no cell phones then. The Coast Guard had radios, but we didn't. By the middle of the night, it was blowing a living gale. The Coast Guard and our rescue team laid up in the lee of Raccoon Island. We then decided we'd go back to Monkey Island and spend the rest of the night there. I later found out that the Coast Guard station at Coinjock clocked the winds at ninety-three miles per hour.

In the deep water between Raccoon Island and Monkey Island, *Rhonda* took a sea across her side just aft of the cabin. I'd never seen anything like that before. When we got to Monkey Island I had to go in the basin because it was too rough to lay to the dock. I told my son Walton to keep the spotlight on the opening to the basin. We had one shot at it, and if I missed, we would be on the bulkhead. I had one hand on the steering wheel and the other on the throttle. We made it. The Coast Guard boys were right behind us. We were all glad to be in there.

The next morning the Coast Guard helicopter found Mr. Simpson at Swan Island. His motor broke down and he had poled through creeks in the marsh to get to Swan Island. The Coast Guard boys found this out on their radio.

When we started back to Waterlily, the helicopter clocked the wind at seventy-two miles per hour. On our way, seas broke on the forward cabin of *Rhonda* three times but the water didn't come in her. I had a lot of faith in that old boat, even if it was held together with old rusty galvanized nails.

Casey Jones

I think this is a good time for me to tell you a little about my old friend, Mr. Casey Jones. Mr. Casey owned the only dock on Waterlily that had deep water right up to the road. He ran a hunting and fishing lodge, farmed a little, had a small store, had a long-net fishing rig and also bought fish.

As I mentioned earlier, when I first rented a space at his dock in the early '60s, my gas boat *Rhonda* had a six-cylinder Chevrolet engine hooked up straight: it didn't have neutral or reverse. You hit the starter and she went, and didn't stop until you cut the switch off. When I first got there, Mr. Casey put me out on the end of Jones Dock. He didn't know if I could handle the boat or not, and he didn't want me to tear up anything. After he found out I could maneuver the boat well, I worked my way up to about third from the head of the dock.

Some days I'd walk in his store and he'd be in what I called "one of those Casey moods." On those days I knew to get what I wanted and get out.

My good friend, Mr. Casey Jones, pauses for a photograph in front of his dock in Waterlily, circa 1957. He ran a hunting and fishing lodge and bought fish in the winter from local long-net fishermen. He also had a fishing rig of his own.

Left to right: Gordon Sawyer and Travis Morris with blind bushes at Jones Dock in 1971—the day Mr. Casey brought the rake.

Casey Jones Dock, Waterlily, North Carolina.

Other days he'd talk your ears off. I spent many hours with Mr. Casey sitting on a bench in the lee of his fish house. When Currituck Sound was full of largemouth bass, I asked Mr. Casey if his men had good luck that day. He answered, "Yes, the sons-a-bitches caught a boatload, and I guess they'll want to come back."

Mr. Casey would let me use anything he had, and I knew he allowed me because I put everything back exactly the way I found it. One day I'd been loading blind bushes there. When I came back in from the sound, there was a rake by the dock. Nothing needed to be said. I knew what that rake was for and I took care of the mess of leaves and branches I had made.

If there was ever a man whose word was his bond it was Casey Jones. If he told you something, it was just as good as if it was sworn to on a stack of Bibles. I always considered him a good friend of mine.

My Guiding Years

I got my first guide's license in 1948 when I was sixteen years old. When folks found out my daddy, a superior court judge, was from Currituck, they wanted to go duck hunting. Daddy always brought men home with him. Our house was like a free hunting lodge and I was the guide. I didn't get paid, but I enjoyed it and got to meet a lot of people. Daddy wanted to be sure I was legal; thus, the guide's license.

I still buy a guide's license every year. I enjoy taking people hunting. Although I don't take people for hire now, I'm afraid that if I don't have one, the game board may decide one day not to let me have a float blind license.

When I was eventually paid to guide, I always tried to carry enough sportsmen to pay the expense of keeping up the rig, or at least I tried to make my wife Frances think that. Frances was a very smart woman who most likely knew what I was up to when I took people out for free, but she went along with it and didn't cause me any grief.

Bill Riddick and I were north of Dews Quarter Island with Bill's float box on a hunting skiff loaded with wood decoys and canvas geese in this photograph from the early '70s.

When I got out of the Coast Guard, I went back to Campbell College. I got out of there in January 1956, came home and went farming. I bought a truck to haul my own produce, but soon found out that to keep hired drivers I had to give them year-round work. This meant that I had to haul produce out of Florida. I soon found myself more in the trucking business than in farming. I pursued these occupations from 1956 until 1970 when I got my real estate broker's license and started Currituck Realty, which I still own and operate as of today. I've always been self-employed, which has allowed me to do all this duck hunting.

In the late '50s, I guided for Mr. Earl Snowden for one or two winters. Mr. Wallace Davis and I ran one of his float box rigs. We were each paid ten dollars a day to hunt geese mostly in the north of Currituck Sound. I was paying two truck drivers twenty-five dollars a day each to drive a nice warm truck when I was out there freezing my tail off for ten dollars, but that's what I wanted to do.

After that, Ambrose "Hambone" Twiford helped me with the float rig. Hambone had a long-net fishing rig, but he didn't fish much until after hunting season. Hambone was the best waterman I've ever known in Currituck Sound. Although he got it from the school of hard knocks, he had what I'd call a doctor's degree on Currituck Sound. When we built blinds at Monkey Island he'd show us where there was another inch or two of water to float the barge. He had poled bass fishermen all around the shores, creeks and marshes of Currituck Sound before the days of bass boats. Hambone was one of my best friends for as long as he lived. Day or night, the weather was never too cold, too foggy or blowing too

My float rig tied out on a bluebird day on the Gull Rock between Waterlily and Corolla in 1974.

hard to go with me in the sound to look for somebody that was lost or overdue. When I'd ask him to go with me, he'd say, "Let me get my foul weather gear."

When we carried sportsmen, we'd put the men in the float box, and then we'd lay off in the gas boat and wait on them. We had a stove in the cabin so it was always comfortable in there. We'd take turns running the boat and sleeping.

Left to right: Walton Morris, Bill Riddick, Paul Lange and Herbert Lange stand aboard *Rhonda* with redheads and canvasback at Jones Dock after a good hunt on Currituck Sound during the late '60s.

Duck Hunting on Currituck Sound

During my guiding days with the Roving Hunters, who you'll read about in the following chapter, the Rovers would hunt the days I didn't have sportsmen. If Hambone was fishing, sometimes one of the Rovers, Fred Newbern, would help me guide. Another man that helped me some was Bill Riddick. Mr. Riddick was head of the farm labor part of the Employment Security Commission in this area. As there wasn't much doing in the winter on the farm, he could get off some to hunt. Mr. Riddick would help me carry men sometimes and sometimes I'd help him carry men, and sometimes we'd just hunt.

The Roving Hunters of the '60s

I had one of the best duck hunting rigs in Currituck Sound, but in order to bring the ducks home you have to have somebody who can hit them. Baxter Williams was a very good friend and fun to be around, but like myself, he was not much of a shot. However, the rest of our group were some of the best shots in Currituck County. Fred Newbern was an excellent shot and probably the best shot from the lay-down box because he could shoot from either shoulder. Vernon Lee Creekmore was also an excellent shot, as was Gordon Sawyer. These fellows and myself were the "Roving Hunters."

The Roving Hunters pose near my house in 1967 after a good hunt for divers south of Dews Island off Webb Marsh. *Left to right*: Vernon Lee Creekmore, Gordon Sawyer, Baxter Williams, Travis Morris, Fred Newbern and guests Jerry Hardesty and James Ferebee.

Getting ready for the hunting season in 1968. *Left to right:* My children, Rhonda, Ruth, Wayne and Walton, load decoys at Jones Dock in Waterlily.

Left to right: Baxter Williams, Vernon Lee Creekmore and Fred Newbern with Travis Morris in the skiff heading to Gull Rock.

Putting men in a float box between Monkey Island and Waterlily at Thompson Rock, mid-1970s.

In the fall when the leaves began to turn and we would wake up to a white frost, we knew we'd soon be hearing the old geese honking. This made the fever start to rise and the boys would start coming up to our house nightly. We would usually have a little Ancient Age or something to liven up the work; however there was never any alcoholic beverage taken into the sound. We didn't believe in mixing alcohol and gunpowder.

We'd go out to the garage and begin painting ducks and geese. They had to be painted and restrung every year. We used them so much that if we didn't restring them every year, the strings would chafe in two by the end of the second season, and the decoys would drift off. We would also have to put new burlap on the wings of the boxes. Finally the time would come to get things loaded up. For this I usually recruited the help of my children.

I had two sixteen-foot shoving poles made for me by Mr. Joe Hayman. I also carried a whole coil of line. When we left the landing with *Rhonda* and that Oldsmobile, we rode until we found the ducks, which was where we threw the anchor overboard. It didn't matter how deep the water was or how muddy the bottom. As Hambone said, "If you want to catch big

Rovers tying out in Morgan's deep water.

fish you have to go in big water, and if you want to kill big ducks you have to go in big water." If the wind was blowing hard, I could anchor the gas boat upwind, fasten the end of that coil of line to the boat's stern, and then let us out to tie out and take up. We ran this rig from Ferebee Island in the north to the Currituck Sound Bridge in the south.

There was a time in the late '60s when a lot of canvasback and redheads were in Currituck Sound. I told the Rovers that I thought we should get my lay-down box out of the barn and go to work on those canvasback. We got the box out, put new burlap on the wings and put it overboard to swell up the seams.

We started hunting up in the north sound in Bellows Bay, Corney Island Channel, Thompson Rock (west of Monkey Island), Gull Rock (between Jones Dock at Waterlily and Corolla) and Morgan's deep water near Aydlett. We were doing well, but I had heard about all the canvasback and redheads south of the narrows. I started riding around and looking through my binoculars for ducks. When I found them, I ran them up and they came right back. I called the Rovers and said, "Boys, I've found the ducks." They were in the deep water east of Ralph Wright's landing and north of Dews Island.

Back to my lay-down box: this is the most deadly ducking rig that I know of since they outlawed the battery. It is made like a coffin. Inside, you lie level with the water. The sides are eight inches high. The deck is fifteen inches wide on the sides, the head deck is twenty inches long and the foot deck is twenty inches long. It has three wings in the front to hold the seas down, with one wing on each side and one at the foot. The wings are covered with burlap so the water can go through them and not make the wings flap. It is no longer in use but remains in my son Walt's museum.

At the time, the Rovers and I used narrow strips of rubber inner tube as bungee cords to hold canvas geese on the wings. It was a one-man rig with all the geese tied up to the head and to the side. You tied a half-moon or "J" with the duck decoys, and it looked just like a raft of ducks. The ducks would come right up the hole and put down at your feet. We tied out ninety canvas geese and two hundred wood ducks. With the box, that gave my twenty-three-foot skiff a load. We nailed a canvasback decoy head on the stem post and painted the name "OLD ROVER" on him.

I made arrangements with the owner of the Walnut Island Motel in Grandy to leave my rig in the canal right in front of the motel. Times were different then. I can't image leaving that rig with all those decoys in there today. We liked the motel because we could eat fried country ham with biscuits and red-eye gravy or eggs and grits for breakfast there and be at our honey hole in just a short while.

Our first day hunting in this location was December 10, 1966. The wind was south by southeast at ten miles per hour, the temperature was seventy degrees and the sky was overcast. We put that rig out and those canvasback and redheads fell right into it, never even circling. My son Walton was with us that day. He was nine years old and had a single-barrel 410-hammer shotgun. He killed one canvasback and was very proud. We soon had our limit. I know if we had stayed there and shot we could have killed one hundred that day.

We usually carried seven people so we could kill enough without going over our limit, which made it worthwhile to tie out all that rig. I don't remember how many days we hunted, but the rig stayed at Walnut Island for seventeen days. We would have our limit and be back to the dock by 8:30 a.m. on many days.

Guides with sportsmen were also out on the sound, watching close by. Picture all those fellows sitting over on the shoal in stake blinds watching us shoot all those ducks while they weren't getting a shot. I told the Rovers that I thought we had worn out our welcome and we had better go back.

I remember the day I left to go back to Waterlily. The sky was overcast. After I came out of the north side of the Narrows it started hailing. I ran up a cloud of widgeon. It almost looked like the old days when ducks would get up and look like a swarm of gnats.

Those widgeon were smart. They stayed in big bunches and were hard to get to come to you in the open sound. We used the two-man sit-up box to shoot widgeon because the only way they would come to a lay-down box was if the wind was southeast: the morning sun was in their eyes and not in yours. We'd tie the lay-down box over near Peters Quarter sometimes and shoot some of those widgeon, but that was a treat I reserved for the Rovers rather than the sportsmen.

As of this writing I am the only living Rover left. The days of the Rovers represented what duck hunting is all about: good friends who enjoyed each other's company.

Sir Thomas Lodge

I didn't keep a logbook in 1971 or '72 because a lot of changes had taken place. By then I had become affluent enough to buy a 1964 twenty-eight-foot Chris Craft Sea Skiff that slept four and had a head and a galley. I had been in the real estate business since 1970 and had started developing Corolla Village for Kenyon Wilson, Carl White and Stewart Hume in the fall of 1971.

The property they owned included the north part of the old Whalehead property, which included Lighthouse Pond and several small islands with good blinds. They let me have the exclusive use of this property over the following seven years until I sold it to what is now the Lighthouse Club. This was a new way of hunting for me. We local people usually had to hunt in the open sound, either in stuck blinds or float blinds.

The season opened December 6, 1973, which was a Thursday. Baxter Williams, Gordon Sawyer, Billy Brumsey and I went to Corolla late Wednesday afternoon aboard the Chris Craft. She was loaded down with gear. When we got to the boathouse at Corolla, we all piled in my Jeep and went out to the Wilsons' oceanfront cottage as guests for the night. Hambone and I had helped to build this house: we hauled all the lumber across Currituck Sound from Jones Dock in Waterlily to the Whalehead Club dock in Corolla. Deputy Sheriff Griggs O'Neal then brought the lumber from the dock to the oceanfront in his six-wheel-drive army truck. In this way, O'Neal, Hambone and I transported all of the lumber for the first two houses ever built on the oceanfront in Corolla.

Kenyon Wilson lived in this house and commuted by boat to Casey Jones's dock, where he left his car to drive to his law office in Elizabeth City. The Wilsons were very gracious hosts. We had a great time with drinks and storytelling before dinner, and Mrs. Wilson always served the most delicious meals.

Thursday morning we woke up early, had breakfast and were out to the blinds. Billy and Mr. Wilson went to Lighthouse Pond and I carried

I took this picture
of the Rovers
during our trip to
Sir Thomas Lodge
in 1971. *Left to right:*
Fred Newbern,
Baxter Williams,
Gordon Sawyer
and Vernon Lee
Creekmore.

Gordon and Baxter to Wood Island. Baxter and Gordon had killed our
three limits by 9:30 a.m. There's no telling how many they could have
killed if I had let them stay. By the time we took up and got back to the
house, we found that Mr. Wilson and Billy had killed their limits before
they came in. When we checked with Walt and Don and Gary Williams
(two of his friends), we found out that they also had killed their limits.
They were hunting the Gray's Island marsh, which I owned at the time
with Bill Riddick and Mark Jester. Most of the ducks killed on the beach
side of the sound were pintail, widgeon and teal. On the west side there
were blackheads and a few mallards.

Another story comes to mind, although I have no written record of it.
The first year that I had the Whalehead property in 1971, I also had the
use of an old house next to the post office, which Dr. Sarah Forbes had
bought. I looked after it and was in the process of trying to sell it for her.
I think it was December of 1971 when I called the Rovers together for
a hunt on the marsh; this was something we were not used to. It was a
blustery afternoon when they all arrived at Casey Jones's dock with their
gear ready to load up *Rhonda.* I had the engine warming up and the stove

Left to right: Gordon Sawyer, Baxter Williams, Vernon Lee Creekmore and Fred Newbern at Whalehead Club's boathouse after a good hunt of mallards, black ducks and widgeon.

going in the cabin, waiting for all hands. We had a bushel of oysters, steaks, eggs and plenty else, including some spirits. Finally everyone was on board: Baxter Williams, Fred Newbern, Gordon Sawyer, Vernon Lee Creekmore and me.

I put her bow eastward, and in about twenty-five minutes we arrived at the boathouse at the Whalehead Club. At that time, I wasn't affluent enough to have a Jeep over there, but I did have an old Corvair. I had paid fifty dollars for it, and on its sides I'd written Currituck Realty with white shoe polish. It took several trips with the Corvair to get all our gear to the house.

Well, we put the oysters on the front porch to stay cool and went inside to light the old oil stove in the living room. This was the only heat in the house. There was a door to the stairway and a bedroom upstairs, and I think maybe two bedrooms downstairs. This place was called "Sir Thomas Lodge" and had belonged to Tom Briggs, who at one time owned the Croatan Hotel in Kill Devil Hills. Dr. Forbes had bought it from his widow. Anyway, we started cooking supper and I went next door and invited my old friend Norris Austin to come over and eat with us.

After supper and more drinks, the place warmed up and everybody got drowsy. Fred and Gordon said they would sleep upstairs. After they went up, we eased the door to the stairs shut so they couldn't get any heat. That night a front moved through and it snowed. The wind blew fifty to sixty miles per hour. Fred and Gordon woke up freezing to death and covered with snow from where the wind had blown it inside under the eaves of the old house. When they found out the stairway door was shut, the words they had for us were not nice!

I think I sat up in the chair all night because I'm scared of mice. In fact, that was the only night I ever spent in that house. It was so cold that it froze our oysters solid on the porch. We had a very good hunt the next day, but I don't remember just what we killed.

My Years at Monkey Island Club, 1974 to 1978

Monkey Island Club was organized in 1869 by a group of men from New York. In 1931 one of the members, Charles A. Penn, bought out the other club members. Mr. Penn was one of the founders of the American Tobacco Company. He lived in Reidsville, North Carolina, and he also had an office in New York.

Edrington S. Penn and Frank R. Penn were the two living children of Charles A. Penn until Ed died in May of 1973. Frank then decided to sell the property. In the process of selling it twice, I opened the club to the public in 1974 and operated it until 1978 when we sold it to the Nature Conservancy. They had no use for the clubhouse, and it has since been vandalized and is falling to pieces. Anyone who wants to learn more about Monkey Island's past should read the history that I wrote for the Currituck County Historical Society's first journal published in 1976. A copy is always on hand at the Currituck County Library in Barco, North Carolina.

Monkey Island was seven acres during the time that I was there. Three miles of beach from Currituck Sound to the Atlantic Ocean belonged with this property as well as several other islands. Mary Island, Raccoon Island, South East Island and Lungreen Island were just marsh islands that had duck blinds on them.

On Monkey Island there was a three-bedroom caretaker's house and the main lodge, which had eight bedrooms and two bathrooms. One had a large, old tub with claw feet and the other had a shower. There was a spacious living room with a big brick fireplace, a dining room, kitchen and large pantry. Upstairs above the dining room were two rooms for the cook and butler. These were not used while I was there. Long, screened porches stretched all the way across the front and back of the lodge.

A furnace provided steam heat and was just like the old one at Currituck School. It originally burned coal and was converted to oil when I was there. The property also had two generators that didn't work. By the time that I was there, Monkey Island had electric power and a telephone.

An aerial view of Monkey Island in 1982.

These four photographs from 1974 show (clockwise from top left) Monkey Island Dock; *left to right*, Hambone and Jack Jarvis building a blind; *left to right*, Hambone, Gene Austin and Jack Jarvis taking a lunch break while building blinds; and Hambone riding on a load of firewood and lumber bound for Monkey Island.

We had these services because when the utility companies wanted to run power and phone lines to Carova Beach, the only way the Penns would let them cross their beach property was for them to run the same lines to Monkey Island.

North of the two houses, the boat basin provided a protective harbor to keep boats during bad weather. There was also a landing house, as we called it, which was used as a workshop and to store decoys. Right in front of the main lodge was a long dock that I had put lights on. We used a little truck that Marcus Griggs made from a Crosley chassis. He made a flat truck bed for the back and put a Briggs & Straton engine on it. When we brought guests in from the gas boat to the dock, we would back the truck down the dock to haul their baggage up to the clubhouse. We also used the truck to haul firewood and anything else that needed hauling.

The Monkey Island Club in Currituck County, North Carolina, circa 1974.

Just to the south of the dock was a little pond inside the bulkhead that I kept some ducks and geese in. I thought it added to the atmosphere to arrive at the dock and see ducks and geese. Swans usually spent the night in a cove on the west side of the island. You could hardly sleep some nights for the noise they made.

When I was there, the club couldn't have operated without Marcus Griggs. He had repaired things on the island for many years, arriving in any kind of weather to fix the furnace or whatever else needed to be repaired. When Ed Penn died, Mr. Marcus and I scattered his ashes over Monkey Island and in Currituck Sound.

The Penns had a battery boat, so called because it was made to haul a battery box (also known as a sink box) back in the days when they were legal. Otis Doe in Wanchese had built the boat in either 1910 or 1916. It was hard to tell by the Coast Guard registration that was kept in the cabin in an Alka-Seltzer bottle. This was before the days of state registration.

The boat was thirty-two feet long and had a little cabin forward. It originally had a mast right behind the cabin with block and tackle to handle the battery. She had a six-cylinder Chevrolet engine and ran pretty swiftly. Although she drew only eighteen inches of water, when she was aground,

Left to right: Ambrose "Hambone" Twiford, Herbert Lange, Shirley Austin and Travis Morris. During the '70s, there were no houses on the beach and only white sand, gold sea oats, blue sky and sea. We'd gather wood that drifted ashore to use for building blinds and always took our fishing rods with us when the big blues were running.

she was aground from bow to stern. We had a 350-gallon tank that we would put in her to haul fuel to the island. We then used a pump to transfer the fuel up to a big tank near the clubhouse.

I tried not to have more than six guests at a time so there was room for Gene and Shirley Austin. Shirley cooked and Gene guided. That also left a room for me. I didn't stay every night but was at the clubhouse every day. Jack and Sylvia Jarvis lived in the caretaker's house. Jack guided; Sylvia helped Shirley in the kitchen and picked ducks.

A long dock at Waterlily, locally known as Penn's Wharf, went with the Monkey Island property. I didn't use this dock. I preferred to leave from

Left to right: Two visiting sportsmen, Gene Austin and Hambone on the dock at Monkey Island in 1978.

Casey Jones's Dock at Waterlily where I had kept a boat for thirty-five years. Jones's Dock was ideal because its dredged, deep harbor water came right up to the road; you could just step out of the car and into the boat.

During this time I owned four gas boats. One was the twenty-eight-foot Chris Craft Sea Skiff that I had named the *Frances M.* after my wife. I used this to carry guests to the island only when the tide was not too low since it had no protection under the propeller if I hit bottom. My main gas boat was the *Rhonda*, which was powered by a 318 Chrysler Marine engine to go in any kind of weather. The third one was the *Corolla Express.* This was a little twenty-foot boat built by Mr. Pat O'Neal in the '50s. It was open with a spray hood and was the only boat I had that was fiberglassed. She had a 225-horsepower Palmer Marine engine and could run thirty-five miles per hour. The fourth was the *Croatan.* This was a thirty-two-foot gas boat with a good-sized cabin and shelter cabin, powered by a Buick car engine hooked up straight. It was built for Mr. Russell Griggs in 1927.

Mr. Russell Griggs owned Hampton Lodge on the north end of Churches Island, which is now Waterlily. They carried sportsmen in the winter. All the important politicians went there to duck hunt. Mr. Russell and his wife Miss Bernnie built the Croatan Hotel, which was one of the first hotels in Nags Head. The same people that hunted at Hampton Lodge went to the Croatan

Travis Morris on Monkey Island Dock in 1976.

In 1979, Mr. Frank Penn leaves Monkey Island for the last time. His attorney, Mr. Charles Campbell, holds the door for him.

Hotel in the summer. Mr. Russell would take the *Croatan* and keep it at the causeway to Roanoke Island to carry hotel guests fishing around Oregon Inlet. There was no road to Oregon Inlet or Oregon Inlet Fishing Center back then.

Gene Austin had a gas boat that was similar to my *Rhonda*, if a little larger. Gene and Shirley lived at Corolla in a house that once sat across the little humpback bridge at the Whalehead Club. They resided there as caretakers for the property even though the old clubhouse was not used at the time. Since there were no paved roads to Corolla, their main transportation to the mainland was Gene's gas boat. They also kept a car at Jones Dock in Waterlily.

When I was there, hunting at Monkey Island was always an adventure. When guests arrived at Jones Dock about 4:00 p.m., I'd greet them and load their baggage on the boat for the trip to the island. From there, the distance to Monkey Island is four miles, and the ride normally took about twenty minutes. We saw large rafts of coot, which are locally known as blue peters, in the middle of Currituck Sound feeding on milfoil. We also saw flights of ducks and geese, which got the sportsmen's adrenaline up.

When we arrived at Monkey Island, Jack or Gene backed the Crosley truck down the end of the dock to load the baggage to take to the rooms. We looked up to the house and saw smoke rising out of the chimney and smelled the woody aroma of an oak fire. As we walked toward the clubhouse, ducks and geese in the nearby pen quacked and honked.

Guests usually stayed three days. After they settled in their rooms and put their guns on the gun rack, it was time for Shirley's hors d'oeuvres. She served steamed shrimp one night, steamed oysters the next and hot crabmeat dip for the third night. Shirley was a great cook and prepared fabulous meals. Afterward, guests lounged around the warm oak fire to spin yarns or watch TV until bedtime. Once in bed, when things got quiet, we had the music of the swan to sleep by.

At about 4:00 a.m., Shirley was up to cook breakfast while Gene and I got the old oak fire roaring. Once done, I knocked on the guests' doors and told them it was time to wake up. After listening to those swans, they were probably dreaming about ducks.

Then I would hear *Rhonda* coming. It was Hambone bringing the guides from the mainland. No matter what the weather, I could depend on Hambone to be there with the guides. We had a table in the kitchen where guides ate. After a big breakfast, guests dressed in their warm hunting clothes while guides warmed up the old gas boats and got skiffs ready to go to the blinds on the beach.

During this time I had control of five miles of beach from Penny's Hill (Lewark Hill) to Great Beach Pond just south of the Whalehead Club. The area encompassed Monkey Island property and the northern part of the old Whalehead Club property, as well as land that now is part of the later established Lighthouse Club. I think I had a total of forty-three blinds.

For every two hunters I provided a guide, a gas boat with a heated cabin and a skiff with a small outboard motor. Each skiff had a plastic box that contained flares, a flashlight, shear pins for the motor and matches stored in a bottle to keep them dry. In those days we didn't have hand-held VHF radios. If anyone broke down, I knew I would be able to find them as long as they had a light.

After guests were outfitted in hunting gear, assigned guides took their guns and shells down to the dock and into their boats. The sound of the exhaust of those old gas boats sitting by the dock idling in the predawn hours, just waiting to go, was music to my ears. Within a short period of time, everyone boarded their boats and headed for the beach. We used gas boats because occasionally it got very rough in the deep water between Monkey Island and the beach. On the occasional slick, calm day the guides just used skiffs. They went mostly to Ships Bay, Parkers Bay or Mary Island. Sometimes they went to Wood Island, Sow Island, Inside Log, Outside Log, Big Fussy, Little Fussy, Birthday Point, Willow Cove or some of the other blinds.

The guides anchored the gas boats off shore and took the skiffs in to the blinds. By about 11:30 a.m., they would bring the men in for lunch. After one of Shirley's lunches, most felt ready for a nap. At around 2:00 p.m. the guides rounded up their men to go back out. We tried to put everybody in good blinds in the morning, but in the afternoon we put them in blinds that were generally not as good. No matter how many blinds you have, there are only so many good ones. You have to let them rest some.

At 4:20 p.m., which was Currituck's legal take up time, the guides began gathering decoys to head back. When guests were in sight of the club and saw smoke drift out of the chimney, their thoughts returned to that warm and crackling oak fire, drinks at the bar, steamed oysters and another one of Shirley's fabulous meals. It was a satisfying end to a long day of duck hunting.

Piney Island Club

W hen I ran Monkey Island Club, Mr. Hammon, who was from Rocky Mount and owned Hammon Electric, brought a group of men to Monkey Island every year. One year he asked me if a young man named John High could visit with his wife, who was also a hunter. The Highs were also looking for a place for their two sons, Robert and Johnnie, to hunt. In between my Monkey Island years and the time that Piney Island was founded, the Highs stayed with Frances and me when they visited Currituck. I took the four of them hunting.

Now to Piney Island, which was founded in 1983. The Midgett heirs owned about 460 acres on Piney Island. It was mostly marsh but had about a mile on the Intracoastal Waterway (ICW). Much of the property was high land because when they dredged the ICW in the 1800s, they dumped the spoil there. Two of the heirs, Mildred Markert and her brother Aubry Midgett, came to my office and asked me if I could sell this property. Aubry got power of attorney, and I listed the property.

I called John High because he was also in the real estate business and told him if he knew anybody that wanted to buy marshland to let me know. John suggested that we put a club together ourselves, and I agreed. John invited a group of men to his house in Rocky Mount, and I went up to meet them. These men became the original members of the Piney Island Club: Don Bulluck Jr., owner of Don Bulluck Chevrolet in Rocky Mount; Howard Cliborne, developer and owner of Kings Grant Realty in Nags Head; John High, developer and owner of a little of everything in Rocky Mount; E.B. Chester, co-founder of Tar River Communications and the only member who flew his own jet and docked his own seventy-two-foot Hatteras Motor Yacht; David Smith, co-founder of Tar River Communications; Lanny Roof, executive with Golden Corral Corporation; DeWitt McCotter, senior partner of Spruill, Lane, Carlton, McCotter & Jolly Law Firm, now known as Poyner & Spruill; Jack Winslow, investor and oral surgeon; Lindy Dunn, CEO of the Guardian Group, which owned nursing homes and had the

The original members of the Piney Island Club, founded in 1983 by John High and Travis Morris. *Front row, left to right:* David Swain, Sandy Thorpe, John Williams, Lanny Roof, David Smith. *Second row:* Don Bulluck, E.B. Chester, Howard Cliborne, Jack Winslow. *Third row:* Travis Morris, Lindy Dunn. *Top:* John High. The members missing from the photograph were DeWitt McCotter, Bill Woltz and Jack Laughery.

franchise for Hardee's in West Virginia; John Williams, CEO of United Federal Savings and Loan in Rocky Mount; Bill Woltz, president of Perry Manufacturing in Mt. Airy, North Carolina, makers of ladies' apparel for many large department stores; Sandy Thorpe, president of Thorpe-Ricks Tobacco Company in Rocky Mount; Davis Swain, developer of housing developments and shopping centers; Jack Laughery, chairman of the board of Imasco, Hardee's parent company; and Travis Morris, real estate broker. We decided to keep the sixteenth membership open at the time.

During our meeting we had agreed to take a look at the property together. Those who were able to come to Currituck stayed with Frances and me. Jimmy Markert, a son of one of the heirs who I later hired as caretaker, helped me show the property since he was more familiar with it. Some of us climbed up a tree to decide on the exact location to build our clubhouse. We closed the transaction at 3:30 p.m. on April 18, 1983.

That same spring, we started construction of nearly a mile of road that led to our building site. Once completed, we built a clubhouse directly beside the Intracoastal Waterway. There are eight bedrooms (two members to each room), four bathrooms, a spacious living room with a big fireplace, a dining

Left to right: Don Bulluck and Fred Dunstan head home after hunting in my float rig in Currituck Sound in front of the courthouse in 1988.

room and kitchen and a large glass room with unobstructed views of the waterway and our impoundments to the north and south. The caretaker's apartment, a utility room, a gunroom and a workshop are downstairs. We have a boathouse with sixteen stalls so that each member has a place to keep his boat. There is also a tractor shed and a brooder house for raising ducks.

Since the club was started, we have always employed a full-time caretaker and cook-housekeeper. The house is cleaned every week, year-round. We can take our wives, children or grandchildren there at any time.

The club eventually bought an additional 160 acres to give us a total of 620 acres, and we have had many good years at Piney Island.

Unfortunately, the first Piney Island clubhouse met with catastrophe on August 23, 2003. JoAnn and I were attending a turkey sponsor banquet in

Our 1996 mullet roast at Piney Island.

In the Piney Island clubroom, my daughter Rhonda Morris looks out the window at the Intracoastal Waterway, my granddaughter Cameron Sawyer reads by the fire, Dubbee Snow scans a newspaper and Jason Swain pauses for a moment on the couch.

Left to right: West Ambrose and DeWitt McCotter tie out a float rig on the northeast point of Piney Cove in 1993.

Left to right: DeWitt McCotter, Travis Morris, Jimmy Markert and David Swain talk about the morning's hunt in 1985. David Swain, who I met when I ran Monkey Island from 1974 to 1978, was one of the original members of Piney Island Club in 1983. We didn't have many ducks at the time, but David was young and optimistic. He would walk the marsh all day and return with usually two or three ducks.

Shawboro. They had just served the meal when I got a call from Jimmy Markert on my cell phone. He said, "She's gone. The clubhouse is burning to the ground right now." JoAnn and I drove straight to Piney Island. It was just before dark and the wind was blowing a gale.

Several fire trucks were at the scene when we arrived. Jimmy had called for help after he realized that he couldn't fight the flames. The Crawford and the Lower Currituck Fire Departments both responded quickly but were unable to save it. There had been a bad electrical storm and lightning struck the wind gauge on top of the chimney. The fire started in the attic and had burned down to the floor. The pilings were all we could salvage. I went home to call all the members and tell them what happened.

We had a meeting and decided to build the clubhouse back just like it was. In the meantime we rented a little cabin from Terry Miles at Midway Marina in Coinjock for the coming duck season, and later, a house beside Coinjock Marina from Louie Davis. JoAnn and I asked Carol Keaton, Piney Island's cook at that time, to come to our house and fix some meals so that the members had a place to talk and relax around a warm hearth. We made it through. By the next hunting season we had a better clubhouse than the one that burned, and the Piney Island Club continues to this day.

Piney Island Club burns, August 23, 2003.

The morning after. *Left to right:* Norman Morse, Fred Dunstan, Jimmy Markert, Travis Morris, David Swain, Bogart "Bogie" Holland.

Piney Island members old and new. *Front row, left to right:* Chuck Wall, Carol Keaton (our cook), Bogie Holland. *Back:* Travis Morris, Fred Dunstan, Judge John Tyson, Don Bulluck, Jeffrey McWaters, Bob Suber and Dom Ronga.

Piney Island rebuilt.

The Ducks Held a Meetin' at Little Oyster Cove

It was Wednesday, December 18, 1991. The weather was getting blustery, and a cold front was predicted to race through the area. I knew DeWitt McCotter was planning to come down on the following night to hunt the rest of the week, but it looked like Thursday was going to be the best day. I called McCotter Wednesday morning and told him that I thought he should come that very evening. He said he didn't think he could because he had a meeting he needed to attend. I told him the ducks didn't know anything about his meetings and that they were going to have a meeting of their own on Thursday. In my opinion, if he wanted to participate he had better arrange to be there. He said he'd think about it and see what he could do. I also called Fred Dunstan and told him the same thing, but he just couldn't come down to Piney Island until Thursday night.

Later in the day, McCotter informed me that he was on the Raleigh beltway and was trying to get things worked out so he could come. I said, "Fine. The ducks are going to meet with you or without you. When you are dealing with ducks, you have to deal on their terms." He called again when it was just about dark and said, "I'm walking out the door. I'll be there by bedtime." I told him that my son Walt and I would see him around 5:30 a.m.

Fred Dunstan later said that he and his wife Diane were out in their yard when they saw McCotter drive by and watched him turn his lights off. Fred told Diane, "DeWitt's going to Piney Island." She said, "No, his wife said he's not going until tomorrow night."

"He's going to Piney Island," Fred insisted.

Walt and I arrived Thursday morning right when McCotter was getting up. The temperature had dropped to about twenty-nine degrees, but the water had not had time to freeze so I wasn't worried about ice. The wind blew northwest at about twenty-five or thirty miles per hour, but I figured we'd be good and dry with that spray hood on my old skiff.

Jimmy had coffee ready, and we had gotten some donuts at the 7-11. While McCotter dressed, Walt and I loaded up the skiff and tried to start the old Evinrude, which had been running perfectly. This time, however, Walt cranked and cranked, but she wouldn't hit a lick. By that time, McCotter had arrived. I told him every time that he went with me in that boat he put a jinx on it; it never starts if he is going. Daylight neared as McCotter paced up and down the dock. We had no other choice but to commandeer Sandy Thorpe's boat. Now mind you, McCotter has a boat, but he may as well not have one because it leaks like a crab float.

The wind howled. I sure did hate to take that ride to Cedar Island Bay without a hood but I knew I had no choice. I got my old Jeep and pulled her in the water. Sandy's boat had a big seventy-five-horsepower Johnson and all his gear was placed inside, neat as a pin. I drove thinking I was going to get wet to the hide, but I was fooled: that boat ran so fast that it was running away from the spray. I kept one hand on the steering wheel and the other on the throttle.

We soon got to Big Oyster Cove, and it was good and light by then. We tied out, got in the blind and then we saw ducks pouring in Little Oyster Cove. McCotter said we should have stopped there. Soon the ducks were coming and putting their feet out to us. I didn't hear any more complaining. It had started to snow and there were continuous thirty-mile-an-hour winds. We decided that with the low tide and strong wind, we'd wait until we had our limit to go out and pick up ducks. I can't complain about Walt and McCotter's shooting. They were very sportsmanlike, and when a big bunch would come in, they wouldn't shoot.

The snow was coming down and the wind was howling. Jimmy's voice came over the radio and asked, "Lorraine wants to know whether we want red-eye or thick gravy, and what time did we want breakfast?" John High had given me a country ham for Christmas that I had sliced and brought over that morning. I had left a note for Lorraine and asked if she would please cook it for our breakfast. McCotter said, "Now boys, that's what I call service."

We soon got our limit. I got mine without even taking my gun out of the case. We poled around the marsh, picked up our ducks and then headed back for the clubhouse with that big oak fire we knew Jimmy would have in the fireplace. By the time we returned, my coat was a solid sheet of ice. I had to dry it in front of the fire.

After breakfast, McCotter took a nap on the sofa by the fire while Walt and I went back to my office to turn the water off. It was getting colder by the minute and I was afraid the pipes would freeze and burst. Afterward, we messed with the old Evinrude a little and finally got it running. We went in the clubhouse and McCotter said, "I think we had better go to Little Oyster

Left to right: DeWitt McCotter and Travis Morris having a great December day in the bush blind at Little Oyster Cove in 1991.

Walton Morris and DeWitt McCotter after a hunt at Piney Island on a relatively dry day.

DeWitt McCotter, with a drink in his hand, asleep on the living room sofa at the Piney Island Club. Note the logbook on the coffee table.

Cove. We don't know what time Fred is leaving Rocky Mount and we've got to beat him there."

We went in my old skiff and Walt, being the youngest, was elected to run the boat while McCotter and I huddled under the spray hood. We had a much more comfortable ride out beneath that hood. When we got to Little Oyster Cove the tide was even lower than earlier that morning because of the steady winds. (Strong north winds always push the water out of Currituck Sound.) Ducks tried to land in the stools while we tied out—no little operation with only inches of water and feet of deep mud. We finally finished and dragged the skiff in the skiffway. Within forty-five minutes after we got in the blind, we had our limit. Now we had to go through the process of dragging through mud to take up decoys. I've never seen anything like it. A blackduck came and landed close enough to shoot while we were out there taking up those decoys.

Just as we came in at around 3:00 p.m., Fred and Dog Lamb drove up and saw us coming. Jimmy said Fred's feathers fell when he told him that we were in Little Oyster Cove. Fred and Dog jumped in Fred's boat and went to Little Oyster Cove. They had their limit by 4:20 and only shot greenhead mallards.

I have been duck hunting in Currituck Sound for sixty-five years, and this was the only day I can ever remember when the ducks flew all day long. Even if the wind is howling and freezing every drop that falls, even if it's spitting snow and the barometer keeps dropping, when the ducks decide to have a meeting, you damn well better be there because they are not going to wait for your meetings!

The Piney Island Dove-Hunt-Turned-Turkey-Massacre, 1989

The morning started as a still gray day, and gray it turned out to be—in more ways than one. Don Bulluck, Fred Dunstan, John High and I sat on the front porch admiring our five turkeys over by the pond. The old gobbler was strutting his full fan and we admired the view so much that we discussed glassing in the porch. Ronnie Capps and Stanley Meiggs arrived about that same time to cook some butts and ribs for lunch. DeWitt and Clint McCotter had left about 4:00 a.m. to go fishing. Tray Bulluck and his friend Wayne Sears got up and ambled out to the porch. Billy Suggs and Dr. Bloom came in about the time the barbeque got on the table. After lunch, Ronnie and Stanley went home as prospects for our planned dove hunt looked slim.

I decided to go down to the *Frances M.* for a little nap. Afterward, I began preparing *Mother Goose* for a ride to Cedar Island Bay. Fred Dunstan walked over to the boat and asked if I had heard the news. I replied, "What news?"

Fred said, "Billy Suggs's dog killed the turkey gobbler."

"You mean that pretty turkey gobbler we were admiring this morning is dead?" I asked.

Fred said, "Yes, he is graveyard dead and already dressed and in the freezer."

I thought to myself, those old hens sure are going to miss that old gobbler, but that's life. Fred told me that Billy felt really terrible about it, but Fred also determined, "He is my guest and his dog has committed this murder."

Anyway, the boys all went dove hunting but there were no doves. John High and I knew there were no doves, so we stayed around the clubhouse and watched boats on the ICW pass by. Just before dark, John and I heard the greatest hollering I had ever heard and then *Bam!* I ran to the door and lo and behold, Billy Suggs's dog had killed another one of our turkeys. When hollering had done no good, Billy had fired his gun to try to get his dog's attention. But that dog had murder in her eyes, and the poor old turkey hen didn't have a chance. Once maybe we can tolerate, but twice in the same afternoon is too much!

I'm leaning beside the cabin of *Mother Goose* at the Piney Island Dock in 1989. In front of me, left to right, are Billy Suggs, Don Bulluck and Fred Dunstan. Wayne Sears is sitting on the side of the boat with John Williams next to him. I can't remember who the sixth fellow is.

About that time, Clint McCotter called from the beach and said for June to cancel the deer meat, they were bringing home wahoo and he would cook it. By the time the McCotters arrived, turkey number two was dressed and in the freezer and the murderer had been put on a string. The McCotters were told about the tragedy, and it was decided that the dog should be prosecuted after dinner. We were then appointed to different positions. McCotter was the judge and I was foreman of the jury.

I had decided, under protest from the judge, that I had better go home before Frances tried me. I told the judge that eyewitnesses had seen the dog commit the murder, and the dog didn't need a trial: she was guilty as charged. I suggested that we give her owner another chance, but that she should be banned from Piney Island forever. Upon leaving I found the dog at the door with the string hanging from her neck where she had chewed loose. I hollered to the judge that the prisoner was loose. I knew if there was a turkey left alive on Piney Island in the morning, I'd be surprised.

Don Bulluck's Special "Bend of the River" Barbeque

W e were preparing for our annual Piney Island Dove Hunt one weekend in 1990, but there was one major problem: we didn't have an official cook. After this experience, we all decided we never wanted to be without one again. I went home that Friday night and complained to Frances about how tired I was from standing up to help Jimmy cook fish. She told me in no uncertain terms that she didn't want to hear it; she had been standing on her feet for thirty-seven years cooking for me!

June Twiford, who cooked for us since our club was founded, had quit to look after her mother and mother-in-law. We had hired Lorraine Wigley to replace her. Lorraine said she would take the job after the weekend because she already had plans to go to Dover, Delaware, for the car races. Don and I then talked on the phone and decided that we should certainly be able to handle the cooking for one weekend. Don said he'd get some special "bend of the river" barbeque, and that Fred planned to pick up some regular barbeque and fried chicken.

As the dinner hour arrived, those present were: Mike Evans and George Collins, who were guests of Fred Dunstan; DeWitt McCotter; Clint McCotter; Don Bulluck; Fred Dunstan; Jimmy Markert; and yours truly, Travis Morris. In the kitchen, I took care of the hors d'oeuvres while Don and Fred prepared their barbeque and chicken. Don told me that while he warmed up his special barbeque, McCotter had been picking in the pot right steady. McCotter had urged, "Boys, you've got to try this stuff. It's really good."

At last, all the food was ready and on the table. We gathered around and Don blessed our scrumptious meal, especially the "bend of the river" barbeque. As we passed collard greens and pepper vinegar down the table, Don kept talking about how this special barbeque was so good and that he wanted everybody to have some. In fact, he talked so much about it that several of us began to get suspicious. The barbeque that Fred brought

Duck Hunting on Currituck Sound

The morning after the "bend of the river" barbeque we went net fishing. McCotter couldn't make it. He was still fighting those chitlins. The Piney Island Club is in the background of this photo.

looked normal, but what Don brought had a distinctly different look. The color was much lighter and it had a different texture than any barbeque I'd ever seen. Don continued to insist how good his special barbeque tasted and that everyone must try it.

For those who don't know him, DeWitt McCotter is a big eater. He's also at the age that it's beginning to show, and his wife Denny won't have that. I understand she arranged to have him dipped in some kind of vat to control his girth. I've heard of dipping cows in a vat to get rid of lice and ticks in the old days, but that was the first time I'd heard of dipping men to reduce their size.

Anyway, when the bowl of special barbeque was handed to McCotter, he scooped a big helping onto his plate and dove right in. He said, "Boys, this stuff is really good," but when that bowl came by me it just didn't look right, so I took only a teaspoonful to be polite. It finally got down to Mike Evans, who has the reputation of being a connoisseur of barbeque. McCotter was right steady stuffing himself, and he had already eaten a load in the kitchen while Don was heating the special barbeque!

McCotter asked, "Mike, what is your opinion of it?" Mike took one bite and shouted, "It's chitlins!" McCotter stopped eating, put his fork down, looked around the table, and asked, "Travis, what is it?" I took a small forkful and when it passed my nose, I knew. If you have ever smelled chitlins cooking, you never forget. Well, I let that forkful get on to my mouth and if ever I had any doubt, all doubt was erased. I confirmed, "It's chitlins but I don't see any corn in them, so I guess they were cleaned pretty good." McCotter groaned, "I have just had enough chitlins to last me till I go to the grave. Pass me some of Fred's barbeque."

After the dove hunt the next morning, we wanted to take the net and try to catch enough fish for supper. McCotter was laid out on the couch. I said, "Come on McCotter, let's go." He replied in all sincerity, "Travis, I just can't make it. I wrestled with those chitlins until two o'clock this morning." And so it was with Don Bulluck's special "bend of the river" chitlins on the night of September 13, 1990.

Duck Hunting at Piney Island with McCotter

It was opening day of duck hunting season on December 15, 1990, and the first day's hunt was over. Members with their guests trickled in, loaded down with hunting clothes and gear. We enjoyed one of Lorraine's good meals while the big oak fire glowed orange and poured out heat. Present were Fred Dunstan and two of his friends from Georgia, Sandy Thorpe, John High, Don Bulluck, McCotter and myself. We thought Howard Cliborne was coming, but no one knew for sure. We decided that McCotter, Sandy and I would hunt together the next day.

I went home and got my clothes ready for the following morning so I could slip out with minimum disturbance to Frances, which she doesn't care for at 4:30 a.m. I awoke at 4:00 and couldn't go back to sleep so I went to Piney Island. When I arrived, I went straight to McCotter's old boat and cranked her up. To my surprise it started, but there was a considerable amount of water inside. She had a little problem of leaking around the rivets. I shut her off and went into the clubhouse.

Howard had arrived and I was told that he was going to hunt with Don and High in Piney Island or Cedar Island Bay. He had already driven down to Piney Island Bay to see if there were any ducks. It was 5:00 a.m. and still dark as pitch. I knew if Howard drove a four-wheel drive down there we wouldn't see him until he walked back or someone went to get him.

High was sitting on the sofa and suddenly said, "We're going to Piney Island Bay regardless of what Howard says." He reasoned that in doing so they would travel with the wind on their way to the blind, and if they got wet during their return against the wind, they'd simply go inside the clubhouse to warm up by the fire. High is always thinking about comfort! Howard then came in and reported, "There are no ducks in Piney Island Bay." Where he went or how he knew, we don't know; but what we do know is that he didn't take that four-wheel drive to Piney Island Bay!

At 5:45 a.m., the wind was blowing a gale out of the north and it was time to go. McCotter elected me to run his boat. When we left the basin, I spotted a tugboat headed north and fell behind him thinking he would break the sea for us. As soon as we got underway, McCotter leaned over to the stern and pulled the plug to let the water out of the boat. We got up to Long Point and had to make a right turn which gave us a beam sea. I kept hollering to McCotter to put the plug in and sit up and get ready for rough water. I got no response and it was time to make my turn. Sandy encouraged me to grab McCotter and shake him, so I took hold of his back and gave him a good shaking. That did the trick.

I don't know how hard the wind was blowing, but those seas were coming straight from Munden's Point all the way down Currituck Sound. It was still so dark I couldn't see anything and the stern light was blinding so I pulled it out of the socket. In the meantime, the old boat was taking quite a bit of water. Then I thought I had seen the point of Piney Island, which designates the turn into Cedar Island Bay. As it turned out, that was not the point and we soon bumped bottom. Remember, big seas were pushing us ashore. As soon as I felt her bump, I knew we were not where we were supposed to have been. I tried to turn her around as best as I could. McCotter was frantically yelling for me to get the boat back in the wind. We both knew that if she got broadside while dead in the water, she would sink. The old motor kept cutting off, but she kept starting before she got broadside. She was on bottom so much that I held my breath, expecting the clutch in the propeller to go out at any second. Then we suddenly hit deep water. We went down the shore a little farther and were pretty sure that we saw the point.

We got into Little Oyster Cove and the seas calmed down but not, of course, the wind. With about one foot of water and six feet of mud, I poled the boat and finally got us tied out. There was only one mishap: a decoy string was caught in the propeller. With all my foul-weather gear on I was extremely clumsy, so there was no way I could reach the propeller without going over face first. Sandy asked, "Who's got a sharp knife?" McCotter replied, "I've got one." Sandy soon took care of the job. My job was to get us safely off the shore in six feet of mud with a little round pole, which I finally did.

After we got the boat in the skiffway, we faced our next problem. A ten-inch-wide, eight-foot-long loose board sat waterlogged about one foot under the water. It was not fastened to anything and just laid there, slicker than a greased pig. Sandy, the most agile one of us, tackled it first. He inched along until he finally got to the blind. Then I got on the

I took this photo of DeWitt McCotter giving Sandy Thorpe orders on how to tie out at the High Blind.

board, McCotter passed the gear to me and I passed it on to Sandy. I told McCotter to leave my gun in the boat and that they could kill my limit. Sandy grabbed my hand and helped me slide along the board. Everything was in the blind but McCotter. He then threw Sandy the bowline and instructed him to tie it onto the blind so he'd have something to hold on to. He finally made it without losing his balance.

Left to right: Sandy Thorpe and DeWitt McCotter wait for legal shooting time at Big Oyster Cove in 2004.

By 6:35 a.m., Sandy had loaded up. McCotter was still messing with his gun. Sandy said, "Take 'em, McCotter." McCotter replied, "I can't get a shell in my gun." I cast my eyes up just a little, afraid to move, and lo and behold, there were five or six mallards about fifteen inches over the decoys. McCotter cussed as he jerked up and down on his gun barrel. Sandy jumped up and killed two ducks. As hard as the wind was blowing, we decided we had best let them drift ashore and we'd pick them up when we were ready to leave. Sandy said, "Get ready, McCotter, here they come." McCotter really got frustrated. He had his middle finger jammed up the magazine halfway to his knuckle. I thought it was stuck in there and that he couldn't get it out. I was really concerned. Sandy said, "Here they are!" I looked and they had just stopped over the decoys. Sandy fired again, but I don't know what he got that time. Worried that I was about to cut it off with my knife, McCotter finally pulled his finger out of his gun.

Still attempting to load a shell in his gun, McCotter removed the barrel. Then he couldn't get it back on. I told him to throw the damn thing overboard, whereupon I got back on that slipping board and worked my way to the boat to get my gun. (My gun is older than I am. It's an old model 11 Remington automatic that belonged to Mr. Joseph Palmer Knapp, the man who started Ducks Unlimited and gave Currituck County more money in 1932 than people paid in taxes.)

I was so aggravated that I forgot to pull my boots up, but luckily I didn't slip off the board. By then, McCotter was completely out of control. He had a shell jammed up in his gun and couldn't get it in or out of the chamber. Sandy and I finally convinced him to put it in the cover and use my gun before some of us got shot. During the course of this entire episode, the ducks were flying. Every time we looked up there were ducks, but McCotter didn't see half of them. He'd been on his knees in the bottom of the blind, working on that gun and saying words I can't repeat here!

McCotter agreed to take my gun, but when the ducks came he wouldn't shoot. He just wanted to blow on his caller. The real problem was that he was afraid he would miss with my gun, and we would rib him. We finally got him to pull the trigger and he found out that the old Remington worked. I didn't know if giving McCotter my gun was a good idea or not. He'd clean her out, throw her to me and say, "Load it, Travis, load it!"

One time after Sandy had shot a duck, I thought that it was going to fall on our heads. I looked around on the water and asked, "Boys, how many do we have now?" Everybody agreed that we didn't know how many, but we had enough. We crossed the board one more time, then poled around the marsh and found seven ducks. They were mallards, widgeons, teal and blackducks. This was no easy job in strong north winds and mud, but at least we could see where we were going on our trip back to Piney Island.

Before we had left the clubhouse to go hunting, there was some discussion about McCotter buying half-interest in Sandy's boat, but a price was never established. Sandy told McCotter he could take it out in legal fees. Sandy said when it got to be enough, he'd start paying the bills. McCotter didn't buy that idea, but every time McCotter's old motor acted up that morning, Sandy smiled and told him the price had increased.

It is important to note that Little Oyster Cove compares with North East Point on Currituck Beach of the old Monkey Island property. It is one of the best blinds I have ever accessed, and that is saying a lot.

There are nearly two dozen good blinds at Piney Island, not including any of the blinds on the ponds.

A hunting trip like the one that Sandy, McCotter and I shared on this day is what has kept me looking forward to the next season throughout the past six decades. A man is entitled to only so many days like that in a lifetime. (My daddy used to say that a man was entitled to only one good bird dog in a lifetime.) December 16, 1990, was a day we'll remember as long as we keep our right minds. That association with good friends, regardless of their walk in life, is what duck hunting is all about.

More Piney Island Episodes

It was the week before Christmas, and all through Piney Island there were a lot of ducks stirring. I called McCotter and Sandy and told them to come down. I thought we might get a few ducks, even though the weather was great for fishing but not duck hunting. After several phone conversations, McCotter arrived in time for one of Lorraine's fabulous dinners. He was supposed to be at two office parties that night: one in Raleigh and the other in Rocky Mount. Since he couldn't be in both places at one time, he told each of them that he had to be at the other place and came to Piney Island instead. Sandy had too many irons in the fire and said he just couldn't make it.

I arrived at Piney Island at my usual time of 5:30 a.m. Jimmy made coffee, then woke up McCotter and a new member, Mike Feasel. After a few rounds of coffee, we decided it was time to go. We wanted to be tied out when it turned light to get the early fly. It was pitch black outside so we used the strong spotlight on my grandson Chandler's boat. McCotter and I headed to the High Blind, which is on the northwest side of Cedar Island Bay. Jimmy followed me until I picked up the pound net stakes at the North End of Piney Island, then he took off ahead of me because his boat is much faster than Chandler's. Jimmy and Feasel were going to the Canvas Point Blind, which is in the southeast corner of Cedar Island Bay.

We followed Jimmy for a while, and then shined the spotlight on the marsh until we picked up the blind. We tied our rig out using a flashlight and then moved a few ducks here and there until we got everything set to suit McCotter. He aimed the flashlight toward our usual entry into the High Blind and I saw a tuft of bull rushes. I said, "McCotter, something is wrong. This doesn't look right." We got a little closer and, lo and behold, this wasn't the High Blind. We looked around until we saw Jimmy flash a light just to the east of us. We knew then that we were in the Middle Blind at the south end of Cedar Island Bay. We have had a lot of experiences,

Travis Morris with his old skiff in the light of day.

but we'd never tied in the wrong blind before. Maybe McCotter's guide was just getting old and senile. We never fired the gun.

Our next episode was of a more serious nature. My grandson Chandler Sawyer, McCotter and I went to Big Oyster Cove one morning and killed one duck. We decided to leave the rig tied out when we came in for breakfast. The sky was clear with the temperature in the high thirties, and the winds were northwest at about fifteen miles per hour.

At about 3:00 p.m., we got in Chandler's skiff and headed back to Big Oyster Cove. The skiff has a spray hood on it and whoever drives has to steer standing up with a stick. McCotter and Chandler were under the hood and out of the wind while I ran the boat standing up. As I headed into Cedar Island Bay, I held onto the spray hood with my left hand and onto the steering stick with my right hand. The thought ran through my mind that if I hit something and the boat dodged, I was holding tight enough that I wouldn't be thrown out.

The skiff ran at full throttle, which was about twenty miles per hour. When I got off against Big Oyster Cove, I didn't slack the throttle because there is grass in there and I wanted to go in on top. I pulled the stick down and I guess I turned the boat too quickly. She slid and then a sea rolled her up. She caught and threw me out so fast that I didn't realize what had happened until I was in the air. It threw me out like a pilot who hit the ejection button aboard a jet, and I remember thinking that I couldn't believe that I was going to get wet. I landed in waist-deep water.

As soon as I hit I saw the boat gone at full throttle, but McCotter quickly recovered from his shock and got back to me. I climbed in the boat and we returned to Piney Island. On the way, McCotter said he got wet from water running down my sleeves. Jack Winslow was on the dock when we came in and noted that when I stepped out of the boat, the expression on my face was one of distress. McCotter and Chandler went back out hunting and I went home for a hot bath and dry clothes.

Had it been in the darkness of morning or had it been in deep water, I probably wouldn't be here writing about it today. It was a lesson that will wake us all up. Even Jimmy bought a new life vest and requires everybody riding in his boat to wear one. I do the same thing. It was a lesson that could save Chandler's life because he saw what could happen. It is his skiff, and by next summer he will be running it by himself. I'm sure the picture of his grandaddy sailing through the air is implanted in his mind for life.

The Rainy Days of January 1992

It had rained for days…weeks, it seemed. I've always hated hunting in wet weather, but if I wanted to hunt in 1992, I had to hunt in the rain. One morning Walt, McCotter and I took my skiff to the High Blind. McCotter and I rode under the hood while Walt ran the boat. When we got to the blind, McCotter said he was sorry we were there because it meant that he had to crawl out from under the hood into the rain. We tied out, and Walt and McCotter got in the blind. I stayed in the boat and pulled up the hood. If I wanted to talk to McCotter, I did it on the radio. He said it was the first time he ever hunted in the same blind with someone and had to talk to them by radio. There was one thing for sure: they were getting wet while I kept dry. They never fired their guns.

By 9:00 a.m., it was raining hard and time for breakfast. I radioed to Don Bulluck, who was at another blind, that we were headed in and that I planned to leave my rig tied out. Don said he was glad to hear me say that because he intended to do the same. Fred Dunstan chimed in from another location and said he would also leave his rig tied out. We returned to the clubhouse and Jimmy had a welcoming oak fire roaring, which felt good to a lot of wet and cold bones. We sat down and enjoyed one of Lorraine's usual good breakfasts. Afterward, everybody fell out for a nap except me. I carried Walt home, worked in my office for a while, and then returned to Piney Island.

Sandy Thorpe had driven in right behind me. He put his hunting clothes on and we both waited in the boat for McCotter. Finally, he came poling down to the dock. We tucked him under the hood and headed for the High Blind. The wind picked up out of the north and it was still raining. Our decoys were not arranged the best since the wind shifted, but we decided to leave them as they were. McCotter and Sandy climbed in the blind and I stayed in the boat. Again, no ducks. We took up at 4:20 p.m. and returned to the club. On the way, I told McCotter and Sandy that I couldn't go with them the next day because I was going to take Jane Dozier's boys. In the

My first wife, Frances Meiggs, and I were secretly engaged in 1953 when this was taken at Women's College, University of North Carolina, Greensboro.

past, McCotter and Sandy didn't have any trouble hunting by themselves, but time changes a lot of things.

Jane's boy, Tater, arrived just before dinner. His brother Charlie was unable to come because he had to work. After we ate, Tater and I went over to Walt's recreation room and shot some pool and played ping-pong. Then we went back to my house and spent the night. It was still raining the next morning when Tater, my son-in-law West and I got to the club. At that time, I learned McCotter had recruited Jimmy to guide him and Sandy. McCotter was just getting spoiled rotten. The duck hunting was just no good in all that rain. After that day, Tater had gone with me twice and not had one good chance to shoot a duck. West had said that if Tater ever went when we had a good day, he would be ruined for life like McCotter and me.

For the record, even if we had a season on geese, I wouldn't shoot one anymore. I've always heard they mate for life. I remember one old goose from 1991 whose mate had been killed, and he just wouldn't leave. He would go from the ponds on the north end of the island to Cedar Island Bay. I think once he came over to Walt's field. Finally, we didn't see him anymore. He probably stooled in to some decoys and got killed. At least that took him out of his misery. I've been there since Frances passed on. I know how that goose felt.

When you live alone after having had somebody to do for you most of your life, only then do you realize what you have lost. Just simple things like if you step on a cricket, nobody is going to come along and pick it up. When your clothes get dirty, if you don't wash them you'll soon run out. If you throw your coat down, nobody is going to hang it up. What I'm telling you is this: when you have a good mate, appreciate her and let her know you appreciate her. Go places and do things that you both enjoy because one day one of you is going to be left alone and then it's too late. Frances and I went and did things we probably couldn't afford, but I have no regrets because if we had waited it would be too late now. I'm a bad one to give advice on investments, but I can give you some good advice on life. Take one day at a time, appreciate what you have and enjoy each day to the fullest because tomorrow you may not have it or you may be gone.

Hunt in South Impoundment: January 11, 1997

The plan was for my son, Walton, and my grandsons, Chet and Chandler, to take Chandler's skiff to North Cedar Island. Walt had seen some blue peters (coot) up there and thought Chet might get to shoot some. My wife JoAnn had to leave by 8:00 a.m. to go to her store so I told her I'd take her along to South Impoundment. I was to pick Chet up at 5:30, but at 4:45 the phone rang and Walt said the wind was blowing thirty-seven miles per hour and the temperature was thirty-six degrees. He said he was not going out in a boat with those boys. I agreed he shouldn't. JoAnn had turned on the outside lights, and it was snowing.

JoAnn was going to drive separately since she had to leave early. I told her I had to pick up Chandler and I'd meet her at Piney Island. I went to Chandler's and everything was dark so I started blowing the horn. Then I got out of the Jeep, went around to his bedroom window and was going to start hollering for him when his bedroom light popped on. Their power had gone out and Chandler's clock hadn't gone off. The kitchen door popped open and Wayne (Chandler's mother and my daughter) started to put words on me for blowing the horn and waking everybody up, but about that time she saw the snow and she calmed down just like rubbing a kitten. Wayne loves the snow.

We caught up with JoAnn on Piney Island Road and went on to the club. Everybody was having coffee and danishes and we joined in. It was still snowing and blowing. When 6:00 a.m. arrived, the boys started getting out. David Swain and Don Fallis went to Little Oyster Cove. Vience, Jim Lilly and Randy Adams went to Big Oyster Cove. Jimmy Markert took Dog Lamb and Allen Ives to Piney Point.

JoAnn, Chandler and I waited until 6:30 and then we took six mallard decoys and two tip ups. JoAnn and I got on one four-wheeler and Chandler got on another one. I really didn't have much hope of getting anything because the day before there was nothing in the South Impoundment. I didn't take a gun. I was just an observer.

My wife JoAnn Morris and my grandson Chandler Sawyer after a hunt in the South Impoundment.

It was still snowing a little when the ducks started coming. It was all pass shooting because they were going across the marsh to Coinjock Bay and were not stooling. The action was fast and furious. JoAnn shot an over and under. She got one with each barrel. Then Chandler made a real long shot. After that, I didn't keep up with who was killing what, but they were both doing good shooting. By then, the air was freezing, but Chandler said his gun barrel was steaming. We stopped at 8:00 and brought in nine mallards. Three were lost in the marsh. Chandler was very excited. He said it was the best day he had ever had in his life.

The snow soon stopped and the sky cleared, but the temperature dropped and the wind still blew hard from the northwest. We returned to the club and JoAnn packed up and headed for her business. Chandler and I hauled up wood for the fireplace because I knew the boys would want to get warm when they came in. Around 9:00 a.m., everybody arrived back for brunch. I had the oak fire roaring. I know that smoke must have smelled good to them when they came in to the dock.

When Vience came in, we learned that Jim Lilly had stepped off the walkway from the boat hide and filled his chest waders with water. They said he got in the blind, took his waders off, rung his socks out and then put them back on. He said he didn't get cold as long as the ducks were flying, but when they stopped, the cold set in. He said when they were ready to leave he had taken about all that he could take.

I don't remember what everybody killed, but they all did some shooting. They were warming up their backsides by the oak fire and sipping bloody Marys when Carol said breakfast was ready. After breakfast, I told them we were going to wait for some fellows from New Jersey to arrive before we went pheasant hunting. Everybody sacked out for a nap.

At noon, the dogs began to bark and I knew that the men from New Jersey had arrived. The CEO of Johnson & Johnson, Dennis Longstreet, Bob Ranki and Dan Gillings were at the door. They came in and, after introductions, went pheasant hunting along with Dog Lamb and Allen Ives. David Swain, Chandler and Jimmy Markert went along without guns to kick up the pheasants and try to control the dogs. The tide was so high the pheasants were not where they were supposed to be. They only got one.

When they returned, Chandler and I loaded decoys on the four-wheelers, rode down to the South Impoundment and tied out while they walked the grounds to see if they could kick up a pheasant. They arrived at the blind by the time we were tied out, and I left Chandler there to call the ducks for them. He didn't carry his gun. Apparently, Chandler was successful with the ducks because they got eight fat mallards. It made me feel good when Dennis told me what a nice boy they all thought Chandler was. He said it was unusual in this day and time to hear a young boy say, "Yes, sir," and "No, sir." I've been taking Chandler to Piney Island since he was about five years old, and I have always been proud to take him.

We went inside the clubhouse and the fellows drove to the nearby Midway Marina, where they were staying, to clean up before dinner. When they returned to Piney Island, Carol had set out hors d'oeuvres of steamed shrimp, deviled eggs, pickles and jalapeno peppers stuffed with cheese. We had a few drinks, then Carol and Marie served a delicious dinner of soft crabs, roast beef, collards, stewed corn, green peas topped with snow peas and lemon pie for dessert.

Up to this point we had enjoyed a nice day. At 7:30 p.m. the phone rang. Jimmy Markert took a call from Jeff Snead. He wanted to use Jimmy's boat to go look for his uncle and some other men who had left Waterlily Wildlife Landing early that morning and not returned. Jeff said they had already notified the Coast Guard in Elizabeth City. We soon heard on the VHF radio that the helicopter had found the boat capsized in the middle of Currituck Sound. There was one man clinging to it who was still alive. We later learned that two other men, two little boys and a dog had lost their lives.

That was an accident that should never have happened. They had no business in Currituck Sound in that little sixteen-foot Polar Craft. I think new people who have moved here find it hard to respect the sound like the older natives. One of these young men and his six-year-old son were natives who should have known better. Johnny Melson was the only one of the group that I knew. And so it was on January 11, 1997.

Goose Hunting with Dr. Gerald Jordan

First, I need to introduce Dr. Gerald Jordan. He is a very well-known urologist with Devine-Tidewater Urology. In addition to practicing medicine, he travels all over the world teaching. I first met Dr. Jordan when he operated on my first wife, Frances, in 1992. She died from cancer that year, but it was not because of anything he did. He was nice to Frances and I appreciated it. I found out he liked to duck hunt and invited him to hunt with me in the fall of 1992. He has hunted with me at Piney Island ever since. Everybody there knows him as "Gerry," and they treat him just like a member of the club. Anywhere else he is Dr. Jordan.

There is only one problem: his schedule stays full so we have to set our hunting dates way in advance. As I've said before, when you are having a meeting with the ducks, you have it on their schedule, not yours. So, when Gerry is at Piney Island, we have seldom had a good duck hunt. The times we have gone, it's either a bluebird day or in between Christmas and New Year's Day when the blinds have been shot out. Still, he usually finds the pheasant hunting good and enjoys the relaxed atmosphere of Piney Island.

On one occasion, Gerry and I decided we might have better luck goose hunting rather than duck hunting. North Carolina had started a September goose season to cut down on the population of geese that don't migrate so we set a date in September of 2004. Gerry, his son Scott and I were going to get some of those geese. Scott is a very pleasant person to be around and he knows how to tie out, which saves his daddy and me a lot of work. On the appointed day, Scott arrived during the late afternoon and I settled him in his room. He later received a phone call from his daddy and of course, Gerry told Scott that he was running late, but was on his way.

It usually works out that Gerry is scheduled to operate on the same days that he's scheduled to come to Piney Island. When he leaves home for the hospital, his hunting gear is already packed in his truck so when he finishes operating, all he has to do is jump in and head for Currituck County. I've had medical professionals tell me that he is a brilliant doctor. It's also worth

Left to right: Travis Morris, Dr. Gerald Jordan and his son, Scott after a goose hunt at Piney Island Bay in September of 2004.

noting that before Gerry was a doctor, he was a carrier pilot in the navy. The best thing I can say about Gerry Jordan is that when you are in his company, he is one of the most unpretentious people that I've ever met. You'd never know his station in life unless you were already aware.

I had noticed on previous mornings a bunch of geese out in the fields near the west side of Cedar Island so after we woke up, had some coffee and a little something to eat, we got in the Polar Craft and headed there. When Sandy Thorpe had gotten out of the club, I had purchased his eighteen-foot Polar Craft with a seventy-five-horsepower Johnson outboard motor. I also bought a pop-up blind to go on it. On account of the McCotter cottonmouth incident of 1992, I don't hunt unless it's in a float blind in the early season.

It was a calm, warm morning. We tied out, then anchored the boat close to the decoys and pulled up the pop-up blind. It wasn't long before we heard the geese coming. We didn't realize that there was somebody tied on the other side of the island until we heard them call the geese. The flock circled around and the people in the other blind shot them. Of course they flared, but one swung by us close enough for Scott to rake him out. We knew that was it for the morning so we picked up and returned to the club.

Dr. Jordan "operating" on a Canada goose in the workshop at Piney Island Club in 2004.

There was another little bunch of geese that I'd been watching down at Piney Island Bay. They went out early mornings and didn't come back until late in the afternoon. They had been roosting on a sandbar right at the mouth of the bay. We decided to try our luck, went down there around 3:30 p.m. and nearly died of heat stroke. We were afraid that if we hadn't gone as early, the geese might have decided to come sooner. We tied out and pulled the boat almost high and dry. Two hours later, we heard the geese coming. Five of them came just like they were headed home, as pretty as you could ever ask for. They swung around from Scott's end, set their wings and started sailing in. When the time was right, I said, "Take 'em!" Scott got two and Gerry got two. In this case, because the other four were already goners, I shot the last remaining goose to put him out of his misery. We had reached our limit for the day and had a very successful goose hunt.

Passing on a Tradition

I started taking my son, Chester Walton Morris, duck hunting with me when he was seven years old. I first bought him a used 410-hammer single-barrel shotgun. Walt was a good shot, but that 410 was almost like shooting a rifle.

One day, Walt was with the Rovers and me when we tied the lay-down box in Peters Quarter. That's just off Currituck Beach, north of what is now Tim Buck II. I had decided that he was big enough to shoot my old Model 11 Remington. Before I could get the gas boat anchored, he had three redheads in the water. I said, "Boys, we have got to get him out of that box before he gets us in trouble."

Mr. Bill Riddick, who had hunted with us sometimes, had a Browning Sweet 16 that he would let Walt shoot. The following Christmas, Daddy and I gave Walt a new Sweet 16 with a gold trigger.

My son Walton and my grandson Chandler coming home with me in *Mother Goose* after a hard day's hunt on Currituck Sound.

As he got older, Walt hunted with me and helped me at Monkey Island Club. I would let him bring along two of his friends, Don and Gary Williams, to hunt there and at Grays Island where I had a camp. They are grandsons of Mr. Tom Brumsey, who was brother to Barbara Smith's father, Mr. Carl Brumsey. Mr. Tom and Mr. Carl were Currituck market hunters when they were young. Mr. Tom was an excellent shot and passed that trait along to his grandsons, but Mr. Carl was like me; he couldn't hit anything.

Walt has quit hunting and now collects decoys. His son Chet wants to go hunting with him so badly, mainly to show his father how well he shoots, but Walt won't go. I think Walt is afraid Chet will show him up shooting.

My oldest grandson, Chandler Reed Sawyer, started hunting with me when he was seven years old. By that time, Monkey Island Club was gone, but I had started Piney Island Club. I've tried to run Piney Island like Monkey Island, the way the old clubs were run. Chandler grew up at Piney Island. The members accepted him and enjoyed his company as well as his talented ability to call ducks. On several occasions, with his Mama's permission, two Piney Island members from Columbia, South Carolina, got him out of school to go hunting with them and call ducks.

When Chandler was a little boy, he'd go across the sound with me to take some of the members in the float box. He would stay with me in the gas

Bert Pooser, Bubba Farr and Chandler Sawyer. We're on our way to Little Oyster Cove.

boat all day and never complain or give me any trouble. I'd let him shoot the cripples.

I bought him an old seventeen-foot wood skiff, and DeWitt McCotter gave him an old thirty-five-horsepower Johnson outboard motor to go on it. I have to admit, the boat is Chandler's, but I'm the one who uses it all the time. It's a 1983 model and still going in 2006.

If I had people I needed to take hunting but didn't have room for Chandler, he had no problem getting a ride. Most of the members were glad to have him go with them and call ducks, but I always told him to let them shoot first. On those occasions when he didn't have a ride I can assure you I made room for him.

I made a mistake with my son Walton. I made him help me tie out the float box many times and didn't let him get in it enough. He hates that float box to this day. I have no intention of making that same mistake with my grandsons. They come first, and then if there is room, somebody else can come.

Chandler has a good hunting buddy, Jeremy Evans, who is an excellent shot. I have taken the two boys hunting often. Even though I can't hit anything, I love to watch those boys shoot.

I gave Chandler my blind in Cedar Island Bay. I had it from the time that I was a boy, but because I'm getting old, I want to assure that my grandsons have a place to hunt. Walt has another blind that I have had since I was young, so my grandson Chet will always have a place to hunt.

Chandler is grown now. He graduated from East Carolina University and married Jennifer Neal, who teaches school in Currituck. At the time of this writing, Chandler works with the North Carolina Wildlife Resources Commission's Educational Facility in Corolla.

My other grandson, Chester Walton Morris, loves to hunt equally as well as Chandler. He has hunted with me at Piney Island since he was seven years old. Chet, who is now seventeen years old, is five years younger than Chandler. I hunted with Chet, Chandler and Jeremy until the year before last.

At that time Chet had a friend, Alex Evans, who wanted to hunt with him. Alex is Woodrow Whitson's great-grandson. Woodrow was a Currituck guide who had a hunting and fishing lodge in Waterlily, North Carolina, called Whitson's Lodge. He was quite a character and anybody that knew him never forgot him. He could spin yarns all day. I told Alex that as long as he lives, Woodrow will never die. He's just like his great-grandfather. I also want to note that Alex always helped me do the work to get the hunting rig ready. Plenty of people will hunt with you if somebody else does the work. Alex helped me and did not grumble. Whenever he wants to go hunting, that boy has a ride with me.

Left to right: Chandler Sawyer with David Swain's son Jason at Piney Island when they were young boys.

Left to right: Chet Morris and Alex Evans with ducks and pheasants at the Piney Island Dock in 2004.

In 2003, there were many blackheads here. Chet and Alex wanted to rig up the float box. That suited me fine. I always liked to hunt with that rig. We hooked my old twenty-three-foot skiff with the float rig on to my eighteen-foot May Craft with a 150-horsepower Mercury and went up to Currituck Shore. The blackheads started coming to that rig and that ruined those boys. They'd never seen anything like that. When the 2004 season came, they were ready to fix her up.

The boys can't hunt the marsh blinds unless I, or another club member, accompany them. Since they both have their own friends to hunt with now, I realized that another boat was required. I personally like to use the old wood skiff but we decided on a twenty-one-foot Carolina Skiff with a 90-horsepower

Left to right: My grandsons Chet Morris and Chandler Sawyer show mallards and teal after a cold day's hunt.

Mercury. Larry Brown made a spray hood for it. (If I have to go in an outboard motor skiff, I at least want some comfort.) Then, Chet and Chandler decided that they needed another boat. With Chandler working in Corolla, and my long-distance trucking runs with Walt to haul produce for his farm market, Chet was the only one of us who had time to spec the boat out and get everything together. Granddaddy just paid the bills. Those boys know I bought those boats for them, but they are in my name. I'm going to keep control so they don't leave me home.

My first wife, Frances Meiggs Morris, went duck hunting with me only one time. It was before we had all these insulated clothes people wear now. Afraid she would get cold, I dressed her up in long drawers and all the clothes

Left to right: West Ambrose, Travis Morris and Walton Morris back from a good hunt at Piney Island.

I could find. It turned out to be a warm bluebird day and Frances almost roasted. When we returned to the dock at Mill Landing, she announced that she had just made two duck hunting trips—her first and last. Throughout our thirty-eight years of marriage, Frances never complained about me hunting. She died of cancer in 1992.

We had four children: Chester Walton Morris, Ruth Travis Morris Ambrose, Wayne Frances Morris Sawyer and Rhonda Lee Morris. Chester married Ginger Davis. Her father owned Coinjock Marina at one time. They have one son, Chester Walton Morris II. Ruth married Marion West Ambrose Jr., whose family owns Ambrose Furniture Company. Wayne married Milford Rodney Sawyer Jr., who is the Currituck County Extension Agent. They have two children. Their daughter Cameron Wayne Sawyer married Eric Lowe and they have two daughters, Ashton Grace Lowe and Cayden Faith Lowe. Wayne and Rodney's son, Chandler Reed Sawyer married Jennifer Neal. Our youngest child, Rhonda, is the director of Kids First in Elizabeth City at this time.

I married JoAnn Hayman in 1995. Jimmy and JoAnn Hayman owned and operated J.I. Hayman & Son Building Supply in Coinjock, North Carolina. Jimmy died in 1986 and JoAnn continues to run and expand the business to this day. JoAnn is ten years younger than me, but I've known her all my life. I dated her sister before I married Frances. I took Mr. Frank Penn's advice after Frances died. Mr. Penn owned Monkey Island when I operated the club. He told me to find a woman that was ten years younger than me. He said if I got one any younger, I couldn't take care of her and if I got one any older, I'd have to wait on her. I took his advice.

JoAnn is a duck hunter. I used to see her with Jimmy at Mr. Casey Jones's dock before daybreak on bad, blustery, sometimes snowy mornings. She doesn't want to go hunting unless the weather is bad. She wants to kill ducks. I remember thinking it would be nice to have a wife that liked to hunt like that. I never had any idea I'd be married to her one day. We never know what life holds in store for us.

JoAnn has one daughter, Jackie, who is married to Lonnie Lee. They have two daughters, Amanda and April. Amanda hunts deer and bears with her father and has hunted ducks with the boys and me. April wants no part of it.

My oldest grandchild, Cameron Sawyer Lowe, is Chandler's sister but not a hunter. She is a horse lover like her father, Rodney Sawyer. My daddy was a horse lover too, but I wanted nothing to do with them. It will be interesting to see if her daughters, Ashton Grace and Cayden Faith, like horses or boats.

Ducks have been good to the people in Currituck since Narrows Island Club was founded in 1883. At their annual meeting in New York City in 1903, a member named Mr. Trotter reported what had been done in the way of purchasing maps and furniture to be presented to the high school at Poplar Branch. Years earlier, many members had regretted the lack of education among the population of Poplar Branch. Some made efforts to encourage their boatmen to learn to read and write, but there were practically no schools on the mainland. Mr. Trotter accepted the responsibility and, along with S.M. Beasley, Colonel Woodhouse and P.Y. Poyner, kept momentum going to lay an educational foundation. As a result of their efforts, the good school in Poplar Branch, named Dr. W.T. Griggs School, is still in use today.

Mr. Joseph Palmer Knapp, who founded Ducks Unlimited, came to Currituck from Brooklyn, New York, in 1917 to hunt ducks. He bought Mackay Island in 1918 and built a large house. He made Currituck his home. In 1932, Mr. Knapp contributed more money to Currituck County than its citizens paid in taxes. Most of the funds went toward school improvements.

JoAnn's granddaughter Amanda Lee with her first swan at Cedar Island Bay in 2003.

The Chathams and Haneses, who owned Dews Island Club, have also helped this county. The Chathams (Chatham Blanket Company) installed lights at the ball field at J.P. Knapp School. The Haneses (Hanes Textile Mills) helped build the Currituck County Library. I'm sure many others, who have been associated with local hunt clubs, have also helped over the years. One recent example is the contribution made by Mr. Earl Slick, who owns Pine Island and Narrows Island Clubs. He gave the Whalehead Preservation Trust over a quarter of a million dollars toward the restoration and furnishing of the Whalehead Club.

The ducks have opened a lot of doors that otherwise would be closed to us Currituckers. All the people previously mentioned came to Currituck for one reason: ducks. Thanks, ducks.

When I grew up in Currituck, locals farmed, fished, worked in the logwoods, drove produce trucks or left to work somewhere else. It was not easy to stay in Currituck. I farmed and was in the long distance trucking business from 1956 until 1970, when I started Currituck Realty. I've been fortunate (or maybe unfortunate) enough to have always worked for myself. At least that has enabled me to do all this duck hunting. I hope I've instilled some of the loves that I have for Currituck County and Currituck Sound in my grandchildren.